I0105114

Jacob Abbott

Light

Jacob Abbott

Light

ISBN/EAN: 9783337266943

Printed in Europe, USA, Canada, Australia, Japan

Cover: Foto ©Thomas Meinert / pixelio.de

More available books at **www.hansebooks.com**

LAWRENCE AND JOHN.

LIGHT.

By JACOB ABBOTT,

AUTHOR OF

"THE FRANCONIA STORIES," "MARCO PAUL SERIES," "YOUNG
CHRISTIAN SERIES," "HARPER'S STORY BOOKS,"
"ABBOTT'S ILLUSTRATED HISTORIES," &c.

WITH NUMEROUS ENGRAVINGS.

NEW YORK:

HARPER & BROTHERS, PUBLISHERS,

FRANKLIN SQUARE.

Entered according to Act of Congress, in the year 1871, by

HARPER & BROTHERS,

In the Office of the Librarian of Congress, at Washington.

OBJECT OF THE WORK.

THE object of this series, though it has been prepared with special reference to the young, and is written to a considerable extent in a narrative form, is not mainly to amuse the readers with the interest of incident and adventure, nor even to entertain them with accounts of curious or wonderful phenomena, but to give to those who, though perhaps still young, have attained, in respect to their powers of observation and reflection, to a certain degree of development, some substantial and thorough instruction in respect to the fundamental principles of the sciences treated of in the several volumes. The pleasure, therefore, which the readers of these pages will derive from the perusal of them, so far as the object which the author has in view is attained, will be that of understanding principles which will be in some respects new to them, and which it will often require careful attention on their part fully to comprehend, and of perceiving subsequently by means of these principles the import and significance of phenomena occurring around them which had before been mysterious or unmeaning.

In the preparation of the volumes the author has been greatly indebted to the works of recent European, and especially French writers, both for the clear and succinct expositions they have given of the results of modern investigations and discoveries, and also for the designs and engravings with which they have illustrated them.

CONTENTS.

A 2

ILLUSTRATIONS.

LIGHT.

CHAPTER I.

RADIATION.

LIGHT proceeding from a luminous object tends to radiate in all directions. If the luminous object is a candle, the rays can only diffuse themselves upward and on the sides, those tending downward being intercepted by the candlestick, the table, and the ground.

If the candle, so shining, is supposed to be at the surface of the earth, or upon any horizontal plane, and there is nothing to intercept its rays *upward or on any side*, then it is plain that the space which the rays illuminate will be of the form of a hemisphere, with a radius equal to the distance through the air to which the light could penetrate. The base of the hemisphere would coincide with the ground, or the horizontal plane, whatever it might be, on which the candle was placed, while the spherical surface of it would extend into the air, forming a great dome over and around the candle, like a kind of lower sky.

Let us suppose that the atmosphere at the time in question is so clear that the light of such a candle would be visible for a distance of half a mile. Then the radius of the hemisphere in the atmosphere which would be illuminated—that is, the distance from the centre to the outer boundary of it, would be half a mile.

But, now, if we suppose that instead of a candle at the surface of the earth we have a flame, or other incandescent object, of the same size, and of precisely the same power to radiate light, in the air half a mile above the surface of the ground, then the hemisphere that was illuminated would become a sphere or globe, the diameter of which would be a *mile*, the distance from the centre to the circumference being on every side half a mile.

The light of this candle, or of the luminous object, whatever it might be, so placed, would be barely visible to any one on the earth looking upward, for, by the supposition, half a mile is the limit of the distance to which the rays could penetrate through the atmosphere and retain sufficient force to produce their proper effect on the human eye. An eye placed any where else, also, on the margin of the illuminated sphere, and directed toward the centre, would see the light. So, also, if an eye were placed any where within the outer boundary of the sphere, and were directed toward the centre of it, it would see the light, the impression being the more vivid as the eye making the observation moved in from the outer boundary toward the centre.

We must not suppose, however, that such an illuminated sphere as we have described would have any precise or definite boundary. Some human eyes are much more sensitive than others, and can see a much fainter light, or, in other words, can see a given luminous object at a much greater distance than others. The eyes of some animals, such as insects, night birds, or beasts of prey, are probably more sensitive than any human eyes. And even beyond the limit at which the light would cease to produce an effect upon any organ of vision, some of its radiations may penetrate and produce other effects of which we have no cognizance. So that the magnitude of the sphere which would be occupied by the radiance would be estimated very differently according to the different tests of the presence of light which we might apply. Still the portion of space that the radiation would fill would in all cases be a sphere, with the luminous source itself in the centre of it, since the limits would be at an equal distance from the centre on every side, whatever might be the test by which the limits were determined.

Thus every luminous point, the radiation from which is not interrupted on any side, is the centre of an illuminated sphere—illuminated *in a certain sense*, as will be presently explained—which sphere is larger or smaller according to the intensity of the light and the transparency of the medium surrounding it. In the case of a common candle, and in an ordinary condition of the atmosphere, this sphere might perhaps be a mile in diameter, supposing the limits of it to be determined by the powers of human vision.

The sphere thus surrounding the luminous point is *filled* with light—that is, filled in a certain sense, which will also, like the sense in which it is illuminated, be presently explained. A light bright enough to be seen at a distance of five miles would in the same manner, if its radiance were not obstructed in any direction, form the centre of an illuminated sphere ten miles in diameter.

The sense in which this sphere is illuminated or filled with light is this, namely, that if an eye is placed any where within it, and is turned toward the centre, it will see the light—that is, there is no part of it in which there would be found any space as large as the pupil of the human eye, and probably not any as large as the area included by the eye of the smallest insect, that would not furnish rays enough to form an image upon the retina so as to produce vision.

And here I must pause a moment to explain how it is

that an image is formed upon the retina of the eye so as
to produce vision.

If you examine one of the glasses of a pair of spectacles
such as are used by elderly persons, and sometimes, indeed,
by persons who are still young, but not near-sighted, you
will see that the glass is thicker in the middle than at the
edges. Such a glass is called a convex lens. If, now, in
the evening, you remove or extinguish all the lights in the
room but one, and put that light at one side, or in one corner, and then proceed to the opposite corner, or into the
darkest part of the room, and there hold a small piece of
white paper against the wall, and one of the glasses of the
spectacles between it and the light at the proper distance,
you will find that an image of the candle, *inverted*, will be
formed upon the paper or card. The image may be small,
but if the experiment is carefully performed it will be beautifully distinct and clear. The lens collects and concen-
trates the light, and forms an image of the candle upon the
paper or the card, which serves as a screen to receive it.
Of course this experiment can be performed on a larger
scale, and in a much more satisfactory manner, with a
proper lens and other convenient apparatus, as shown in
the following engraving.

Now in the eye there is just such a lens and just such a
screen—that is, just such in *respect to function*. The lens
is in the front part of the eye, and the screen, which is
called the *retina*, is in the back part; and it is by means
of this image on the retina that the picture of the outward
object is conveyed to the mind.

Now when it is said that the whole of the illuminated
sphere surrounding a source of light as described is, in a
certain sense, *filled* with light, the meaning is that there is
no part of the whole space where an opening no larger
than the pupil of the human eye will not take in enough to

THE INVERTED IMAGE.

form, by their concentration upon the retina, an image of the luminous point from which they proceed, just as a lens, held in the manner I have described, will gather rays enough coming from the candle on the other side of the room to form an image of the candle on the paper screen.

"Lawrence," said John, one day, as he had been reading about this in a book, "here's a nice experiment for me to try, if I only had a pair of spectacles."

"Would my eye-glass answer the purpose?" asked Lawrence.

"No," replied John, "I think not. I suppose your eye-glass is concave, and what I require is a *convex* lens. Let me take it a moment, and I can soon tell."

Lawrence was lying, or, rather, reclining on a sofa in the corner of the room near a window, with his head toward the window, so that the light fell fair upon the page of the book which he was reading. John was sitting at a table near. Lawrence unhooked his glass from the cord to which it was attached, and handed it to John, saying at the same time,*

"There it is; but find out whether it is convex or concave with your eyes, if you can, and not with your fingers."

"Why not with my fingers?" asked John.

"You can feel of it if you find it necessary," said Lawrence, "but the less we touch polished glass with our hands the better. There are always particles of dust floating in the air, and these alight on our fingers and on the glass, and when we rub our fingers over the glass we rub the surface with these."

"And does that do any harm?" asked John.

"It depends upon what the particles of dust are composed of," replied Lawrence. "Some of them are minute fragments of cotton or woolen fibres worn off from clothes. *They* would not do much harm. Some are minute spores of plants."

"What are *spores?*" asked John.

"A kind of seeds," said Lawrence. "They are from such plants as form mould and mildew; and some smaller still —so small, indeed, that the plants themselves can not be seen except with a microscope; and you can judge how small the seeds must be. These would not do much harm any more than the woolen and cotton abrasions. But there is another kind of dust which comes from the road, and which consists of minute scales of iron, from the shoes of the horses, and the tires of the wheels, or, what is still worse, of fragments of stone from the pavements, some of which are *siliceous*—that is, of the nature of flint, and are exceedingly hard. When you rub these over the glass with your fingers, or with a cloth, or a piece of leather, although no one rubbing produces any perceptible effect, after a time the fine polish begins to be dimmed.

* See Frontispiece.

"So that, if you are going to study optics," continued
Lawrence, "and are to have any nice lenses and prisms to
make experiments with, I advise you to be very careful
how you rub them with dusty fingers or dusty cloths."

"Yes, I will," said John.

"A good lens," said Lawrence, "is a very delicate thing,
and sometimes a very costly thing. It requires, in the first
place, a very nice preparation and mixture of the materials
out of which the glass is made, and great care in the making of it, to secure its being uniform and homogeneous
throughout, so as to act upon the light in the same way in
every part. Then it is a very nice operation to grind it
precisely to the true form, and to polish it perfectly. So
that, when you get a good lens, if you ever do get one, you
can't be too careful of it."

While Lawrence had been saying these things, John had
been attentively examining the eye-glass, without, however, touching the glass at all.

"Yes," said he, "yours is a concave lens; it is thinner
in the middle than at the edges. I want one which is
thicker in the middle than at the edges."

"Perhaps the landlady will lend you her spectacles,"
said Lawrence.

Lawrence and John were at this time in lodgings in London. The keeper of the lodging-house where they had
taken their rooms was quite an elderly woman, and very
soon after he had given Lawrence's eye-glass back to him,
John heard her footsteps in his bedroom, which was a
small room adjoining their sitting-room. John went in
immediately, and asked her if she used spectacles. She
said she did sometimes. John asked her if she was willing
to lend him her spectacles a few minutes; he wished to
make an experiment on light with them.

"Certainly," she said. He could have them as well as

not; but they were a poor old pair, very loose in the joints, and she was afraid they would hardly be of any use to him.

John said that the looseness of the joints would not be of any consequence. So the old lady went out and pretty soon returned with the spectacles.

John's plan was to go into his own room to try his experiment, as it would be necessary to darken the room, he said, and he did not wish to interrupt his cousin's reading. But Lawrence said he would like to see the experiment himself. So John lighted a candle and closed the shutters, following the directions given in his book. Then, placing the candle on one corner of the mantel-piece, and going to the farther corner of the room, with the spectacles and one of Lawrence's cards in his hand, he attempted to form an image on the paper in the manner we have already described.

CHAPTER II.

WONDER AND MYSTERY.

JOHN was quite surprised at one phenomenon which presented itself to his attention in performing his experiment. While he was making his preparations, Lawrence remained on the sofa, intending, as soon as he found that John had succeeded in bringing the light to a focus and producing an image of the candle, to go and see it. But John seemed to encounter some difficulty, and presently he said that he could not manage the spectacles, for he could not keep the *bow* out of the way.

"If I take them by one of the glasses," he said, "and hold the other glass up for the light to shine through, the upper bow falls down over it, the joints are so loose."

"Never mind," replied Lawrence; "let it fall."

"Then that will make a blank bar across my picture," said John.

"No," replied Lawrence; "try it and see."

So John held one of the glasses up, with the bow belonging on that side hanging down over it, and then, placing his card against the wall, he moved the glass to and fro, so as to find the right distance for producing a distinct image. He expected, of course, that the shadow of the bow would be seen extending from above down over the picture, if he succeeded in producing any picture.

But, quite to his surprise, he soon obtained a very excellent image of the candle, and without any shadow, or dark bar, or any other indication of the bow at all, to disfigure it. The image was reversed, it is true—that is, it was upside down—but it was very distinct and very beautiful.

There was the flame perfectly formed, though pointing downward, and the wick (which appeared like a slender black line in the middle of it), and the top of the candle (which was rendered bright for a little distance by the translucency of the wax at the margin), all plainly to be seen.

John was very much pleased to find his experiment so successful, and he called Lawrence to come and see it. Lawrence came, and he showed John how he could vary the effect by changing the distance of the lens from the candle, though this made it necessary also to change the distance from the lens to the screen. The nearer the candle was to the lens on one side, the farther it was necessary to place the screen on the other, in order to bring the rays to a *focus*, as it is called—that is, to make the image distinct.

John was, however, very much surprised to find that there was no dark line across the picture of the candle corresponding to the bar formed by the bow of the spectacles. Lawrence told him it would be the same with any opaque substance at the surface of the glass. He might put a patch directly upon the glass itself, and it would not show as a spot of shadow on his picture.

John tried this experiment. He cut out a small round piece of paper about as large as the section of a pea, and then, wetting it to make it adhere, he put it on the glass. Notwithstanding what Lawrence had told him, he could not help expecting to see it produce a round black spot upon the image of the candle. But it did not do so. The image became somewhat less bright than before, it is true, but there was no appearance upon it of any shadow, either from the bar or from the paper patch.

Lawrence explained to him how this was, and I intend to repeat the explanation in a future chapter; but now I must return to the illumined sphere, which, I have said, always surrounds every luminous point, so far as there is no object intervening to intercept the rays.

This sphere, as has already been said, is filled with light in the sense that in no part of it can an eye be placed where there will not be rays enough, if the eye is turned toward the luminous point, to enter the pupil and form an image of the source of the light on the retina, as John formed an image of the candle on his card by the lens. And it is in this sense only that the space within the sphere is illumined, namely, that it is completely filled with rays of light proceeding in close proximity to each other from the centre to the circumference.

These rays, it is true, diminish in intensity, in some mysterious way, as they proceed from the centre to the circumference; but, in whatever way this diminution of intensity is effected, it is *not* done by a separation of the rays from each other as they diverge, *so as to leave some parts of the space empty.*

Radiation from a luminous point is, indeed, often in books represented by lines diverging from each other as they recede from the centre, and this, however closely the lines are together in the centre, gives us the idea of a necessary *separation between them* toward the outer portions. But we must not imagine that the diminution in the intensity of light, as the distance from the source increases, is produced by any *separation* of the rays. Exactly how we are to picture this diminution of intensity to our minds it is difficult to say, but it is certain that it is not the result of the *separation of lines of radiance from each other* as they recede, leaving intervals between them dark.

In describing the phenomena we use the word *rays*, and we represent the radiation by lines; but we must conceive of it, so far as we can, as homogeneous throughout, and as diminishing in intensity, when it does so diminish, without the least interruption of continuity.

The sphere thus is illuminated only in this sense, that an eye in any part of it, turned toward the centre, would see the light; looking in any other direction through the sphere, it would see nothing. We may, however, conceive such a sphere to be illuminated in another sense, as follows:

If, for example, the spherical space were filled with dust or smoke, or any other substance consisting of fine particles, and if the light in the centre were increased in intensity just enough to make up for the loss that would be occasioned by the intercepting of the light by such particles, then the space included would be illuminated in another way. The sphere itself would then become visible, just as the sunbeams do when shining through a crevice into a dusty or smoky room, or the rays of the sun when they illuminate the mistiness floating among the clouds at evening in the western sky, and which people call "drawing water," under the erroneous idea that those lines of light are streams of vapor ascending into the air. The effect is produced by the rays of light passing through the interstices in the clouds, and then shining upon and being reflected by the particles of mist which they meet with on the way. It is true that the direction of the illuminated lines is generally downward, as there is usually more mistiness in the atmosphere near the earth than above, though they are sometimes seen ascending as well as descending, as is represented in the following engraving.

If now the sphere surrounding the luminous point which I have been describing were illuminated in this manner— that is, by having particles floating in the air to receive and reflect portions of the light—with a sufficiently increased intensity at the source to just make up for the loss, the form and the extent of it—that is, of the whole

ILLUMINATED VAPORS.

sphere—would be visible to the eye, appearing like a vast ball of light a mile in diameter, bright at the centre, and gradually diminishing in brightness from the centre to the outer surface, where the light, by insensible gradations, without any definite boundary, would melt into the darkness and disappear.

It must be understood, however, that this sphere would be thus visible to us, not by means of any of the rays of light which were passing out from the centre to the circumference of the sphere on their regular course, but only by means of that portion of them which was intercepted on the way and reflected to the eye by the solid particles.

And this brings to our minds a principle of fundamental importance, namely, that no light produces any effect upon our vision except such as passes *into the eye.* It may pass before us or across our field of view in any quantity and of any intensity without being perceptible to us at all. It is only when it *enters the eye,* and falls upon the screen called the retina, in the back part of it, that we can have any consciousness of its presence.

Thus, if such a candle as we have supposed were surrounded by an atmosphere so far transparent as not to contain any substances capable of sensibly reflecting the light, the light would go on diminishing in intensity as it receded from the centre until it disappeared, and in that sense the whole sphere would be illuminated—that is, it would *be filled with a radiation of light;* but in looking toward it we should see nothing except the luminous point in the centre, and we should not see that unless our eyes were turned directly toward it.

And now let us suppose that, instead of *one* luminous point or candle flame, there were two, and that they were placed at the distance of half a mile from each other; the two illuminated spheres would then interpenetrate each other, so to speak, to the extent of half their diameters. The rays from A, proceeding in the direction toward B, would encounter those of B coming toward A. The encounter would be *direct* on the *line joining the two central points*, and in all other parts it would be indirect, and the crossing would be at various angles.

ILLUMINATED SPHERES.

In those parts of the space common to both spheres which are equidistant from the two centres, the two radiances encountering each other would be equal. In those parts which were nearer to one than to the other, the light coming from the nearest point would be strongest. Thus the radiances issuing from the two centres would encounter each other, in the space common to both, at every possible angle and with every possible disparity of force.

And yet, so far as we can discover, such rays do not interfere with each other in the least; for, wherever you put your eye within the portion traversed by the light from both the centres, if you turn your eye to either, you have its image as clearly and distinctly painted on your retina as if the other did not exist; that is to say, the radiance which comes from one of the points, though its track has been crossed all the way by the emanation from the other —both *filling the space completely*—is not disturbed or interfered with by the other in the slightest degree.

This is wonderful, and it is for the purpose of furnishing a clear, simple, and precise idea of the nature of this mystery, as the foundation of a right understanding of what is to follow, that I have made these suppositions of candles in the air.

If you have followed what I have said closely enough to have received distinctly an idea of the *nature* of this wonder of the non-interference, in the ordinary sense, of luminous emanations moving in contrary directions, and crossing each other at every possible angle and on the same track, you are prepared to appreciate in some degree the amazing magnitude and extent of it. Every star in the sky is the centre of a sphere that is illuminated by its radiation in the manner I have explained—a sphere, too, which is so enormous in extent that its magnitude and grandeur surpass all human conception.

Light is proved to move at the rate of between one and two hundred thousand miles in a second, which is sufficient to carry it round the earth in the *seventh part* of a second, and there are stars so remote that it would require *hun-*

dreds of years for their light, moving at that inconceivably great velocity, to reach the earth! Think of the enormous magnitude of a sphere traversed by the radiance of such a star! Now every one of the millions of stars—and if we include, as we ought to do, with those that can be seen by the naked eye, those which are brought to view by the tel escope, either as single stars or are resolved from nebulæ, the number is to be reckoned at thousands of millions—is surrounded by a sphere of radiance which must extend to us, and all these spheres occupy the same space, entering into, crossing, and interpenetrating each other in every direction, so that, when you hold up a needle in the evening air on a clear night, there are millions upon millions of distinct radiations passing through the eye of it in both directions, encountering each other at every possible angle and with every conceivable disparity of force. And yet each one of these radiations maintains its way so entirely uninterrupted and undisturbed by the rest, that you can select any one of them you choose, and, by conducting a sufficient portion of it from the space around, by means of the telescope, to your eye, you can there produce a picture of its source upon the retina as clear, and distinct, and as sharply defined as if its own radiance was the only one emitted, and had the entire and exclusive occupation of the field.

There is no way of escaping from or diminishing the unutterable wonderfulness of these facts. I have only called the emission a radiance — that is, something radiated — without intending to say in what it consists. It *has been* thought to consist of streams of infinitely minute particles of matter. It is now generally considered as an undulation or vibration in some extremely subtle medium diffused through space, to which the name *luminiferous ether* has been given, which phrase means, simply, the unknown something which transmits the light. It is supposed that one or the other of these two suppositions must be correct, because these are the only two ways in which we can conceive that action of any kind can be conveyed through space. But whether there may not be modes of transmission for force that man, with his present mental constitution, can not conceive of, is a grave question.

At any rate, it is now universally agreed among scientific men to regard light as transmitted by a series of undulatory movements in an intervening medium, and all the calculations and all the language used in describing the phenomena are based at the present day on this hypothesis. In all the drawings, however, and other illustrations intended to represent the action of light to the eye, the radiation is represented by lines, which are more appropriate to the idea of a progressive motion of streams of particles than to that of undulations. We are obliged to use both these modes, as the best symbols of thought at our command; but when we attempt to pass from these symbols to the realities which they are intended to represent, we are lost in wondering what the actual nature of emanations can be that can thus meet, and cross, and encounter each other in every imaginable way—in such countless numbers, within such inconceivably narrow limits, and at such inconceivably rapid rates of motion—and each of the millions of separate motions pursue its own way without being in the least degree deranged, disturbed, or interfered with by the rest. We ask ourselves in amazement, What can the emanation be, in its intrinsic nature, that can exist under such conditions as these? What is light? We can not tell. We can really know nothing of its essential nature. We can only study such of its modes of action and such of its effects as come within the reach of our senses and of our half-developed reasoning powers.

CHAPTER III.

THE VELOCITY OF LIGHT.

It may seem strange, as, indeed, it really is, that, since light moves at such a velocity as to carry it seven times around the earth in a second, there can be any possible way by which its velocity can be measured. But many ways of doing this have been discovered or devised.

Some of these methods are astronomical—that is, the velocity of light is determined by observations of certain movements and appearances among the heavenly bodies, and by computations made from them. Fully to understand these computations, and the astronomical principles on which they are based, requires a degree of mathematical and astronomical knowledge which few persons have time to acquire. But astronomers have given such abundant proof of the soundness and trustworthiness of their methods, in the exactness—to a second—with which their predictions in respect to eclipses, transits, occultations, and other celestial phenomena are always fulfilled, that when they agree in assuring us that they have determined any point connected with celestial phenomena, we have every possible reason for placing confidence in the result.

A general idea, moreover, of one of the methods adopted can be obtained by the aid of the following engraving. The method consists in making first an exact computation of the time when some astronomical phenomenon will actually occur, and then observing the difference in the time in which it is seen to occur by an observer on the earth when the earth is on opposite sides of its orbit. The phenomenon most convenient for such purposes as this is an eclipse of some one of the satellites of Jupiter.

VELOCITY OF LIGHT—ASTRONOMICAL DETERMINATION.

In the engraving, *e* represents the satellite about entering the shadow of the planet. The precise moment at which it really enters is known beforehand, and it is found by accurate observation that the apparent time of its entering, as seen from the earth when it is at T, in that part of its orbit which is nearest the planet, is a certain number of minutes sooner than when it is observed when the earth is at *t*—that is, in the part of its orbit which is most remote. From these data, the time required for the light to pass through the diameter of the earth's orbit is determined.

The conclusions deduced from astronomical observations like these have been abundantly confirmed by ingenious devices which have been contrived for measuring the velocity of light on the earth's surface. The engraving on the following page represents one of these methods, the principle of which, with a little attention, can be easily understood, though it would require a great deal of practical experience and skill, and very delicate powers of observation, to enable any person to perform the experiment successfully with it, so as to arrive at a satisfactory result.

You will see by the engraving that the apparatus consists of two separate parts, which are connected by dotted

VELOCITY OF LIGHT—EXPERIMENTAL DETERMINATION.

lines. In using it, the two parts are placed at the distance of several miles from each other, the separation being represented by the break in the dotted lines. The left-hand part of the apparatus is simply a hollow tube, having at the right-hand end of it a lens, and at the other end a mirror, which are so adjusted that a beam of light entering through the lens shall be brought to a focus on the mirror, and then reflected back through the lens again on the same path by which it came in.

That an incoming and an outgoing radiation can thus pass through the same tube, in contrary directions, at the same time, without in the least degree interfering with or deranging each other, is only another example of the wonderful action of this mysterious power that was described in the last chapter.

The portion of the apparatus toward the right is set at the place where the observation is to be made, the other part, as has already been said, being placed at as great a distance as possible, but within view. This second part of the apparatus, like the other, consists of a tube, with a branch near one end of it, which is open toward the source

of light.   As the light enters the tube, the rays, of course,
are diverging.   Near the entrance they pass through a
lens by which they are made parallel.   A little farther on
they pass through another lens, by which, from being parallel, they are made to converge, but before coming to a
focus they strike the plate of glass, M.   This glass, though
not strictly a mirror—not being silvered on the back—reflects a large portion of the rays, turning them into the main
tube, but without, however, changing their convergency.

On the other side of the tube is a system of clock-work
moved by a weight attached to a cord that is wound round
a drum seen at the end.   Those who are interested in
tracing out the connections of machinery will see that
there are four axles in this work.   The first is the axle of
the drum.   Near the end of this axle, toward the right, is
a large *toothed wheel*, which carries a small wheel upon the
end of the next axle.   On the left-hand end of this second
axle is another large wheel, which carries a small wheel on
the third axle.   This same system of large wheels carrying
small ones is carried through the fourth and fifth axles,
and thus a very great velocity is imparted to the fifth by
the descent of the weight.

On the left-hand end of the fifth axle is a large wheel,
which you see enters into the tube through a slit made in
the side of the tube for admitting it.   The margin, or circumference of this wheel, is cut into alternate *notches* and
teeth, square in form and equal to each other, and the wheel
is so adjusted in respect to the tube at the point where the
beam of light passing through is just coming to a focus,
that each tooth, as it moves by, shall stop a beam of light,
while the notch that follows shall allow it to pass.   Thus,
when the wheel is rapidly revolving, a succession of flashes
will pass out through the tube, following each other with
inconceivable rapidity.

Let us now suppose for a moment that the weight is disconnected from the drum, but that there is a handle attached to the axis of it, by means of which we can turn the wheel at any rate of velocity we choose. Let us also suppose that the other part of the instrument—that is, the part that we placed on a distant hill, is so far away that it would require *one second* for the light to pass over the adjoining country to it, enter the tube, be reflected to the end of it, and return. This would be impossible in fact, since light travels at a rate which would carry it *seven times round the earth* in that time. We can, however, suppose it for the purpose of illustrating the action of the apparatus. Let us suppose that we allow a flash to pass out through a notch, and that an observer with his eye at A is watching for its return. At the expiration of the second, the time required for its journey, he would see it through the glass, M, which, it will be remembered, was not silvered, but only polished, so that, while it reflected a portion of the light, it also allowed a portion to pass through.

But if, on the other hand, the wheel were to be moved while the ray of light was gone, so that, on the return, it should find a *tooth in its way* to stop it, instead of an opening to allow it to pass through, it is plain that the eye at A would see nothing. And, moreover, if the wheel were made to revolve regularly at a rate which should bring a notch and a tooth alternately into the path of the ray at intervals of a second, then every flash which went out through the notch would find a tooth in its way to intercept it when it came in, and the eye at A would not see the light at all.

If it required less than a second, as, indeed, it actually must, for the ray of light to pass to and fro, then all that would be required to stop the flashes on their return would be to make the wheel turn faster; and it is easy to see that, from the degree of speed which it would be found necessary to give to the wheel in order to bring the teeth up rapidly enough into the path to stop every flash on its return, it would be easy to determine the time required for making the journey. You will see, by a careful inspection of the figure, that there are two little indexes at the ends of the fourth and fifth axles, by which the speed of the wheels in this instrument is registered, so that the computation can easily be made. The result of a trial made with the apparatus near Paris corresponded very nearly, in respect to the velocity of light, with those which had been obtained by the astronomical calculations.

I have described this contrivance in detail, both because it is very useful to learn to understand the nature and action of mechanism from engravings and descriptions, and also because this case is a striking instance of the ingenuity and skill which have been exercised by scientific men in discovering secrets of nature which we might have thought it hopeless to attempt to unfold. The idea of attempting to find any means of actually measuring, within a space of a few miles, the velocity of a motion swift enough to pass seven times round the earth in a second, would have seemed to every one, at first view, to be utterly chimerical.

Do not forget the result, which is, that the velocity with which light moves is such as to carry it about 175,000 miles, or seven times round the earth, in a second. The rays require about eight minutes to come to us from the sun.

CHAPTER IV.

THE LAW OF THE SQUARES OF THE DISTANCES.

I MUST admit that the title of this chapter is not, at the first view, at all an attractive one.   It sounds very mathematical.   But then there is an interest and a beauty in a mathematical principle when it is once understood, and as this one, known as the Law of the Squares of the Distances, can be easily understood when properly explained, and as it is one of fundamental importance, not only in its application to the subject of light, but in countless other cases where we may observe its operations in the phenomena of nature, I hope that none of the more intelligent and thoughtful of the readers of this book will be alarmed at the mathematical aspect of its name.

The circumstances under which John's attention was first called to it were somewhat curious.   He and his cousin Lawrence had been making an excursion that day to the Tower of London, a famous old structure, which was used in former times as a fortress to defend the city from hostile vessels coming up the river.   Of course, since this was its object, it was below the city at the time when it was built, but the city has now extended far below the spot on which it stands.   It is, for other reasons also, now useless for any purposes of defense, but it is still preserved, and is used as a museum of curiosities, and contains vast collections of ancient arms and armor, and of a great many other relics of old times which are very curious to see.

Lawrence and John had been to visit it that day, and had stopped on their return to their lodgings to dine at a coffee-house; for, as it was uncertain what time they would

return, they had concluded not to make arrangements for
having dinner at home. It was eight o'clock when they
arrived, and, when they went into their sitting-room, the
housemaid went before them and lighted the candles which
stood on the table in the middle of the room. They were
two very tall candles, in two very tall candlesticks, so that
the flames of the candles were about two feet above the
table.

John went to the sofa and sat down upon it, as if he
were glad to find a place where he could rest.

"I'm tired," said he, "and yet I've an hour's work to do
before I go to bed."

"How is that?" asked Lawrence.

"Why, I have a half hour more of study to do, and then
it will take me full half an hour to write about our visit to
the Tower in my journal. I must not let my journal get
behindhand."

In order to explain John's remark that he had half an
hour more to study that evening, I must relate how it was
that he came to make this voyage to Europe with his
cousin. His cousin had just graduated at the scientific
school, and had formed a plan to go and spend some
months in Paris, in order to pursue still farther certain
branches of science for which there were great facilities in
that city, and also to visit and examine certain great engineering works which had been constructed in England and
France. He was, in fact, educating himself to be an engineer.

John, when he heard of his cousin's design, felt a strong
desire to accompany him. He proposed the plan to his
mother. She was at first somewhat surprised at the proposition, but, the more she thought of it, the more she was
pleased with the idea. She said that she would speak to
his father about it.

When she proposed the plan to her husband the next morning at breakfast, he at first shook his head somewhat doubtfully, saying, "It will make a great interruption in his studies."

"It will help him very much in his French, at least," said John's mother.

"True," said his father; "it will help him decidedly in his French."

"And it will be a great advantage to him every way," said his mother, "to see a little of the world."

"And then, besides," said John, "I can go on with my studies in other things. Cousin Lawrence is an excellent teacher."

"Can you study while you are traveling?" asked his father.

"Yes, sir," said John, promptly. "I can have my book and study my lesson in the cars just as well as any where else. That would not prevent my looking out of the window now and then."

"Well," said his father, after a moment's pause, "I'll see. Talk with your cousin about it, and see what he says. Form a definite plan, and show it to me, and I will consider it."

So John went that same day to find his cousin, and brought the question before him. His cousin seemed very much pleased with the idea of having John for his companion, and said that he would draw up some kind of a plan in the form of conditions, and that then, if John agreed to them, he could offer them to his father.

A few days after this, Lawrence presented a paper to John containing the conditions, asking him to examine them and see if he was willing to agree to them, or whether he would wish to have any alterations made. John examined the conditions attentively. There was only one alteration that he suggested, and that was, that in the article which specified that he was to study so much every day, the words *Sundays excepted* should be inserted. Lawrence said that was meant to be understood, but that it would be better to have it expressed. So the words were put in. Some other minor changes were also made.

"And now," said Lawrence, when the last interlineation was made, "we are ready to pass it to be engrossed."

"What does that mean?" asked John.

"To have a fair copy made," said Lawrence. "In legislative bodies, when they have made all the amendments and alterations they wish in any proposed law, they *pass it to be engrossed*—that is, to have a fair copy made, in a plain hand, so that it can be easily read. When this copy is made they have it read again, and, if it is all right, they pass it *to be enacted.*"

The paper expressing the proposed agreement between Lawrence and John, when engrossed, read as follows:

"I propose to take John Wollaston with me to Europe, with his father's and mother's consent, on the following conditions in respect to his studies:

"1. That he is to study three hours every day, subject entirely to my direction, Sundays excepted.

"2. He is never to intermit his studies on account of traveling, whether on foot, by railway, or by steamer.

"3. He is never to ask to be excused from his study on account of his not feeling well. If *I* think he is so unwell on any day that he ought not to study, it will be my duty to say so.

"4. Time spent in reading attentively such books as I shall direct, answering questions in respect to what he has read, writing notes and abstracts of the same, and listening to additional explanations from me, is to be reckoned as study hours. Time spent in writing letters or journals, or in reading books chosen by him for his entertainment, is not to be so reckoned.

"5. The whole responsibility of keeping an account of the time, and of seeing to it that he studies three hours every day, devolves on him, and not at all on me.

"6. He may gain to the extent of one hour for any particular day, if he wishes, by studying over his time on the preceding ones; but if he falls short of his time any day, he can not make it up on succeeding ones.

"7. Inasmuch as all human plans and arrangements are subject to unforeseen and unavoidable difficulties and interruptions, an allowance is made of one day each fortnight for failures. If the accidental failures do not exceed this number, the engagement on his part will be understood to be faithfully kept.

"8. In case of failures greater in number than this, or in case of general remissness and neglect on his part in the fulfillment of his duty as herein stipulated, there is to be no penalty whatever, except the loss of credit which he will sustain as a young man to be relied upon for honorably fulfilling his engagements.

"LAWRENCE WOLLASTON.

"Agreed to by me,
    "JOHN WOLLASTON."

John's father, when these articles were presented to him, read them very attentively. John stood by watching him, to observe the effect.

"The penalty does not seem to be very heavy," said he.

"Now, father," said John, "I think it is very heavy indeed. I would not lose my credit with my cousin Lawrence for honorably fulfilling my engagements on any account whatever."

READING THE ARTICLES.

Mr. Wollaston was glad to hear John say this, and, after some farther consideration and reflection, it was decided that John should go. And it was under the operation of this agreement that John had half an hour more of study to provide for before he went to bed, on the evening of his return from his visit to the Tower, as described at the commencement of the chapter.

But I have occupied so large a portion of this chapter in explaining the nature of the agreement between Lawrence and John, and the circumstances under which it was made, that the explanation of the law of the squares of the distances must go over to the next. I shall, however, let the title stand; we shall come to the subject in due time.

CHAPTER V.

CANDLES TOO TALL.

" I wish they would not have such tall candles and candlesticks in our rooms," said John, as he took his seat at the table. " The light is away up in the air, and I want it down here on the table, where I am going to write."

So saying, John began arranging his books and papers on the table, looking up, at the same time, with an expression of dissatisfaction on his countenance, toward the light. He, however, made no more complaint, but said,

" I am going to do my half hour's study first, and afterward write in my journal. I want to do the hardest first."

" I advise you to write in your journal first to-night," said Lawrence; " I have a particular reason, which I will explain to you by-and-by."

John was quite inclined in all cases to follow Lawrence's advice, as he had always found his " particular reasons" very satisfactory. So he wrote for half an hour in his journal, while Lawrence sat near, in a large arm-chair, reading the papers.

As John shut up his journal and prepared to commence his half hour's study, he looked up at the tall candles again.

" It would have done just as well," said he, " if these candles had only been half as high, and then I should have had twice as much light."

" *Four times* as much," said Lawrence.

" Twice as much," said John; " they would have been twice as near, and so would have given twice as much light."

"Being twice as near," said Lawrence, "would make them give *four times* as much light. This is a case in which the law of the squares of the distances comes in. The square of two is four."

Lawrence explained this principle to John as follows:

"Light, as we all know, spreads itself in both directions as it recedes from the luminous point—that is, laterally, which means from side to side, and also up and down. If it spread only laterally, then the same light would, at double the distance, fall on *double the space*, and would consequently be weakened one half. But it spreads *in the other direction also*—that is, up and down; so that at twice the distance it will spread over four times the space."

"That is curious," said John.

"Yes," said Lawrence, "and it is more curious still, as it is only a single case of a universal law. The two surfaces that the same portion of light from a candle would shine upon at different distances are *similar*, in the geometrical sense. Do you know what the word similar means, in a geometrical sense?"

John said he supposed it meant alike, or somewhat alike.

"It means *exactly* alike in *form*," said Lawrence, "without any regard to *size*. Thus an egg and a ball are similar, *in common language*, being both rounded, but they are not similar in the geometrical sense, because they are not *exactly alike in form*. A globe made to represent the earth, if it was made a perfect sphere, would, in common parlance, be similar to the earth. It would be made, in fact, expressly in resemblance of it, but it would not be similar in a geometrical sense, for the earth is not a perfect sphere.

"So with surfaces. Two kites of exactly the same size and nearly the same shape would be similar, in common language, while, on the other hand, if, of these two kites of exactly the same shape, one was only a little toy an inch long, and the other were *six feet* long, we should not ordinarily say that they were similar. We should say that they were very different. In a geometrical sense, however, they would be similar, while the two that differed in form, however slightly, though of the same size, would not be similar.

"Now," continued Lawrence, "if we cut a square hole in a piece of paper, and let a light shine through it upon a card, or sheet of paper, for a screen, held behind it, the bright spot made on the screen will be similar to the opening, provided the screen is always held square to the light. The *size* of the bright spot would, however, be very different at different distances, and the law of increase would be as the *squares* of the distances—that is, at twice the distance it would be four times as great; at three times the distance, nine times as great; at five times the distance, twenty-five times as great, and so on in all cases."

"I mean to try it," said John.

So saying, he rose from his seat, and, procuring a card, cut a small square hole in the middle of it. He then put one of the candles away in the closet, reserving the other to form the source of light. The hole which he made in the paper was about an inch square.

He then put the reserved candle on the floor, and near it placed a chair. On the chair he placed a big book, on one end, in such a manner that he could slip the card between the leaves at the other end, by which ingenious contrivance the card was supported at about the height of the candle. He placed the book so that the card should be at the distance of a foot from the light, and then held a sheet of white paper at the distance of another foot. He found, as Lawrence had said, that the bright spot was two inches in dimension each way, making the spot illuminated by the light on the sheet *four times* as large as the hole through which the light came.

"We might know that it must be so," said Lawrence, "since the rays of light proceed in straight lines, and so diverge from each other at the same rate at every distance. It follows from this that, since that portion of rays which pass through the square hole have diverged from each other one inch in passing *one foot* from the source—and those that pass through the hole must do exactly that— they will diverge from each other two inches in passing through two feet. This will, of course, make the bright spot twice as long, and also *twice as wide*, for the divergence is the same in both dimensions, and thus the bright spot will be four times as large as the opening through which the light passed to make it. By the same reasoning, if the distance were three feet, it would be nine times as large, for the bright spot would contain three rows of spaces as large as the opening, and there would be three spaces in each row. If the distance were five feet, the illuminated space would be twenty-five times as large as the opening. And so in all cases. The space illuminated by any particular portion of the light from any point will be as the square of the distance; and as the intensity of the light, supposing that none of it is lost, would be diminished just in proportion to its diffusion, the intensity upon any given *space will be inversely as the square of the distance*."

The principle is the same, whatever is the form of the opening through which the light shines, whether square, or round, or of any irregular figure. Whatever the shape of the opening may be, the surface that it illuminates will be of the same shape—that is, mathematically similar, and it must be enlarged, so far as it is enlarged at all, in *two* dimensions—that is, in what the mathematicians call a duplicate, or double ratio.

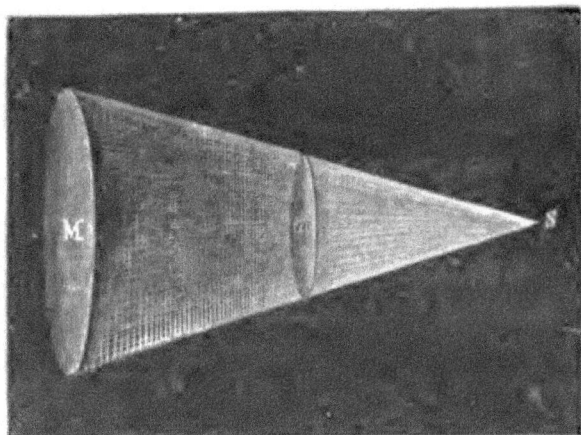

ENLARGEMENT AS THE SQUARES OF THE DISTANCES.

Thus, in the engraving, if the distance from S to M is twice as great as from S to *m*, M will be doubled *in two dimensions*, and will, consequently, be four times as great as *m*.

John was much interested in the experiment which he had made, and still more in the general statement of the law which it illustrated. It is, indeed, very useful to know this law, as our action in certain cases will be much influenced by it. And few persons, unless they have had instruction on the subject, are aware of it. It is true that every body knows that the nearer we are to the light the better we can see; but it is not every body that knows *how much* better—that is, every one is not aware that by diminishing the distance *one half* between the light and his book, he makes the brightness of it upon the page *four times* as great as it was before.

A gentleman who had occasion to travel much in country places where he often found it difficult to obtain a good light for certain work of writing which he had to do, had a flat tin box made of an oval form, about four inches by three, with a socket for a short candle near one end of it on the inside. He also had a paper shade, which could be fixed to the candle, to throw the light down upon his paper. By this arrangement his light was brought within six inches of his paper, and as the effect was nearly doubled by the reflection from the inner surface of the shade, which was white, his one candle flame threw nearly as strong a light upon his paper as eight candles would have done at the ordinary height of one foot. It would have given as much light as four candles without the shade, on the principle above explained of the law of the squares of the distances.

The cover of the box was made of the same form with the bottom of it, with a socket in it, also near one end. By this arrangement the sockets did not interfere with each other when the cover was put on, and the gentleman, if the light from one candle, near as he brought it to the paper, was not enough, could at any time have two, the box serving as one candlestick, and the cover as the other. The

PRACTICAL RESULTS.

C

two would, of course, give him as strong a light *on his paper* as sixteen candles at the ordinary height would have
done.

Lawrence talked with John about the law of the squares
of the distances for some time, showing him that it applied
to all cases of the emanation of any force from a centre,
such, for example, as heat and gravitation; and this for the
simple reason that the force, or influence, whatever it might
be, in receding from the centre, was expanded in two dimensions, length and breadth, and so the surface within
which any given portion of it was included was *enlarged*
in two dimensions, which caused the surface to increase
not simply as the distance, but as the square of the distance. And as the intensity of the influence would be diminished just in proportion as it was diffused over a greater space, the intensity—that is, the force at any one point,
would be *inversely* as the square of the distance.

This principle of the very great difference in the brightness of the light at different distances from the source of
it—a difference far greater than one, without understanding the principle, would suppose—is of great importance
for all who have to do any work by artificial light, as, in
many cases, by diminishing their distance from the light,
they can gain a much greater advantage than they would
at first imagine.

There is another principle, also, which it is very important to understand, and that is the illumination of the paper, or the page, or whatever else it is that the light shines
upon, depends not merely upon the distance, but also upon
the angle at which the rays fall.

This will be plainly seen by the engraving on the opposite
page, which shows that when the same book is held obliqua-
ly, as it is at the left, it receives but half as much light as
when it is at right angles to the rays, as shown on the right.

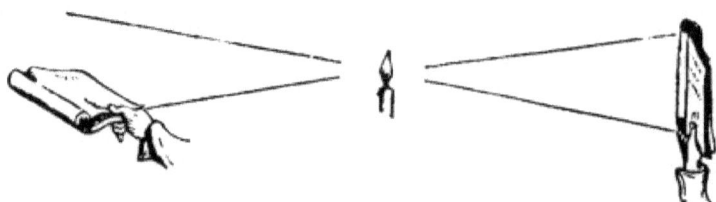

DEGREE OF ILLUMINATION.

Lawrence, moreover, explained to John that this same principle of the effect of an increase in two dimensions, in respect to any quantity, had a very wide application. It applied, in fact, to all *similar* surfaces—that is, similar in a geometrical sense. If, for instance, we have two rooms, and one is twice as long as the other, but is of exactly the same shape—that is, if it is twice as great in all its other dimensions, it will take, not twice as much, but *four* times as much carpet to carpet it. A person, without reflection, might have said that it would have taken twice as much; but, with a little consideration, we see that if it had been twice as long and *only just as wide*, it would have required double the quantity of carpeting, but, being twice as long and twice as wide both, it will take four times as much.

It makes no difference what the shape of the two surfaces may be, provided that they are of similar shapes. A boy has a kite a foot long. He wishes to make one of the same shape two feet long. It will require four times as much paper. If he requires his new kite to be three times as long as the other, and every thing in proportion, it will require nine times as much paper.

So with the covering of a ball. There will be four times as much leather in the covering of a foot-ball ten inches in diameter as there would be in one of five inches; for the square of five is twenty-five, and the square of ten is one hundred, and one hundred is four times twenty-five.

It is true that the diameter of the balls are not *lines in the covering,* but that makes no difference. The areas of surfaces are as the squares of any *corresponding lines*— that is, any lines bearing the same relation to the two surfaces compared.

Lawrence explained these things to John, who listened with close attention, and asked many questions, and at length said,

"Now take your pencil and write what I shall dictate to you, to be copied into your book of notes."

So John took his pencil, and Lawrence dictated as follows:

"FUNDAMENTAL PRINCIPLE.

"In all cases of force or influence of any kind radiating from a centre, and not intercepted on its way, the intensity at any point is inversely as the square of the distance from the centre."

"And now," said John, after he had written this, "it is high time for me to begin my half hour's study."

"But your half hour's study is over," said Lawrence.

"Over?" said John, surprised.

"I think so," said Lawrence. "Let me see."

So saying, he took out his watch and said, "Yes, and ten minutes more. Listening to instructive explanations from me, you know, is to be counted for study, if you listen attentively and try to understand them."

"Good!" said John, in a tone expressive of great exultation; "I thought I should have half an hour more of arithmetic before I could go to bed; but now I can go to bed at once, for I am tired and sleepy."

So saying, he put away his books and papers, and prepared to go to his room.

"But, Lawrence," said he, "what was the particular

reason you had for wishing me to write in my journal first ?"

"It was because I was going to explain to you the law of the squares of the distances in relation to radiation for your study this evening, and I thought you would like your journal work done first."

"Yes," said John; "I am very glad that you planned it so."

CHAPTER VI.

INTENSITY OF LIGHT.

THE art of measuring the intensity of light is called *photometry.* The word comes from the Greek word *photos,* which means *of light,* and the word *metros,* measurement. On the same principle, the word photometer would mean a light-measurer, just as thermometer is a *heat*-measurer, and barometer a weight-measurer, and dynamometer a strength-measurer, from Greek words meaning heat, weight, and strength.

Some very curious devices have been contrived for measuring the comparative intensity of different lights. In some of these devices the observation is made by examining the shadows cast by the two sources of light to be compared. How this is done is shown by the engraving. There is a stand with an upright rod (m) fitted to it, and beyond the rod a screen, made usually of a plate of ground glass, to receive the shadows. Any white surface would answer well enough for such a screen, but ground glass is found to possess some peculiar advantages for this purpose.

The two lights to be compared are placed at a distance from the upright rod on the side opposite to the screen, so as to cast the shadows a and b upon it.

In the engraving the sources of light are a lamp (L) and a candle (B). The shadows seem to be of nearly the same intensity. If, on careful examination, they are found to be as nearly as possible alike, and if the lamp, as would seem to be the case, is nearly twice as far from the screen as the candle, then it would show that the light from the lamp

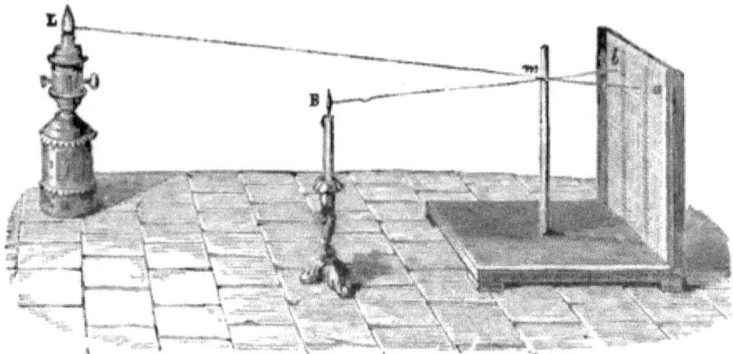

COMPARISON OF SHADOWS.

would be nearly four times as great as that from the candle. Of course, by exactly measuring the two distances
and squaring the numbers expressing them, the exact ratio
would be ascertained.

It would be found, in using this instrument, that if, instead of a lamp at A, candles of the same kind as the one
at B are used, and if the distance of A from the bar m,
which intercepts the light, is made double that of B, there
must be four candles at A to make the shadows equal.

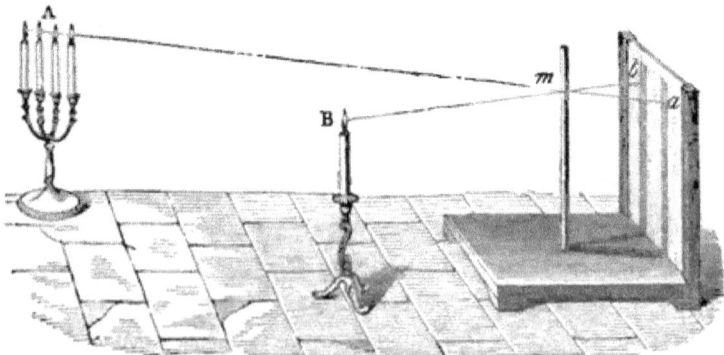

LAW VERIFIED.

There have been various other methods devised of measuring the comparative intensity of light. One more I will
describe.

COMPARISON OF LIGHTS.

It is represented in the engraving, where you see on the
left a screen similar to the one in the last figure, being
made of a plate of ground glass set in a frame.   From the
centre of the plate there extends forward a shade or screen
of *black pasteboard*, which divides the ground glass plate
into two parts, and confines the light coming from each of
the two sources that are to be compared to its own side of
the screen.   In the engraving, the light shining on one side
of the screen is seen to come from a jet of gas, while that
on the farther side is the light of a candle.   On the table,
in lines extending from the glass to the lights, are scales
of inches, or other equal divisions, by which the distances
of the lights from the glass respectively can be at once
determined.

Thus one half of the glass plate is illuminated by one
light, and the other by the other, and, by looking at the
two parts from the outer side, a very exact comparison
can be made between them.   One or the other of the
lights must be moved until the two illuminations are pre-

cisely equal, and then, by observing the distances at which the two lights are placed, and squaring the numbers representing them, we get their relative intensities.

Another instrument still, which helps to show how many methods have been devised to accomplish this purpose, is known as Ritchie's Photometer.

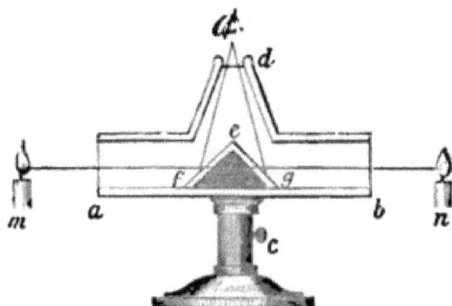

RITCHIE'S PHOTOMETER.

The engraving shows it in section. It consists of a box (*a b*), with openings on the opposite sides for the admission of light from the two sources that are to be compared. In the centre, above, is a conical tube, open at the top at *d*. Here the eye of the observer is to be placed to compare the effects of the two lights, which shine upon two slopes of white paper, *e f* and *e g*, which come together at *e*. One light or the other is to be moved until the degree of illumination produced by them upon the paper is the same. The intensity of the radiance, then, from the two sources will be in proportion to the squares of their distances from the centre of the box.

Instruments constructed on these principles, but quite complicated in their details, are fitted up in gas-works to determine the quality of the gas. In France the intensity of the light is estimated by comparing it with that furnished by a certain amount and quality of oil burning at a certain rate per hour, and in England the standard of

comparison is the light furnished by a certain kind of candle. The lamp or the candle is placed upon one scale of a
balance, with the proper weight in the other scale. The
gas-burner is placed by the side of it, and the issue of gas
is so adjusted as to make the two lights equal, as shown
by the photometer placed near. Both lights are then allowed to burn until the scale containing the lamp or candle rises, showing that the prescribed amount of oil or of
spermaceti has been consumed. The gas is then shut off,
and the metre shows how much gas has been consumed.
By this means the quantity of light which the gas affords
per cubic foot is easily computed.

Photometers, besides being useful in determining the
light-giving power of different kinds of candles and different qualities of gas, have also been employed in comparing
the light coming from various other natural and artificial
sources. Those who have made these observations have
come to the conclusion that the light of the sun is equal
to that of between *fire and six thousand* of the standard
candles, when placed at the distance of eighteen inches;
that is, that to throw a light equal to the full blaze of the
sun upon a sheet of paper would require the combined
power of no fewer than five to six thousand candles placed
at the distance mentioned. Of course it would be practically impossible to place that number of candles so that
their light could be combined. The experiment only shows
what number would be necessary if the combination were
possible.

As for the light of the moon, even when full, every one
knows that it is vastly inferior to that of the sun, but few
are aware how very much inferior it is. The experiments
of scientific men with photometers, and the computations
which they have made from their observations, vary con-
siderably in their results, as was to have been expected,

but the average of them makes the light of the sun about *five hundred thousand times* as great as that of the full moon on the brightest nights. Of course this can only be considered as an approximate result, as it would be impossible, with the means yet devised, to estimate such enormous differences of intensity between two lights with much accuracy.

CHAPTER VII.

CANDLES AND LAMPS.

THERE is a very near and intimate relation between heat and light. Both come together from the sun, and both are subject, in many respects, to the same laws. In other respects, the modes of action which they present are strikingly different. The prevailing opinion among scientific men at the present day is, that the phenomena of heat and of light are produced by the same agent, modified in its action in some mysterious way, the secret of which has not yet been discovered.

We shall see, in another chapter, the curious relation which heat and light bear to each other, as they come to us together in the radiance of the sun.

One of the most striking differences between heat and light is, that heat can be absorbed by any substance and afterward given out again slowly, but light, *apparently*, is not subject to this mode of action, except in a few special cases, and in these only to a very limited extent. If you put a brick or any other substance in the rays of a hot sun, or before a bright fire, it will absorb the heat, and then, if afterward you take it to a cool place and hold your hand before it, you will feel the heat which it has absorbed radiating from it and warming your hand; but if you take it into a *dark* place, your eye will not detect any luminous radiance from it—that is, there will be no evidence to the senses that it absorbed light as well as heat, so as afterward to emit it. But perhaps we can not certainly infer, from the fact that our senses do not detect any such radiance, that there can not be any. It is conceivable, certainly, that the two kinds of radiance may be absorbed and afterward emitted together, and that the hand is much more sensitive to the one kind than the eye is to the other; in other words, that the radiance, acting as heat, will produce the sensation of warmth in the nerves of feeling while its intensity is yet low, and yet will not, acting as light, produce the sensation of vision in the nerves of sight until its intensity is very high.

However this may be in the case of radiance of low intensity, we know that, when the radiance is of high intensity, the heat and light bear a very intimate relation to each other, so much so that the degree of heat is expressed often by the kind and intensity of the light that is emitted. Blacksmiths and machinists say "red hot" and "white hot" to indicate different degrees of temperature, and also "cherry-red" and a "low red in the dark."

There is a curious difference between solids and gases at high temperatures in respect to their power of *emitting light.* When any substance is so intensely hot that it emits bright light, we say that it is *incandescent;* when a gas is incandescent, it forms flame. Young persons, often, in looking at a flickering flame blazing up from the fire, or at that rising from a candle or a lamp, wonder *what it is.* Now it is simply incandescent gas—a kind of inflammable air called hydrogen gas, which, in burning—that is, in combining with the oxygen of the air—is heated to such a degree as to become incandescent.

Burning is simply a chemical action. It is usually the combining of some combustible with the chemical substance called oxygen. There are certain very curious considerations connected with the fact that so much heat is developed by the combination of oxygen with combustible substances, but I have not space to explain them here. All that is necessary to enable the reader to understand what I am going to say about light is, that combustion is a process that develops great heat, and that the intensity of the heat depends in a great measure on the rapidity and abundance of the supply of oxygen.

The intensity of the *light* which is developed by the heat depends, in a great measure, on the substance heated consisting of *solid particles*, for, at the same temperature, the particles of a solid substance are found generally to emit a stronger light than those of a gaseous one. But then, on the other hand, certain gaseous substances emit a greater degree of *heat* in combustion than most solid ones.

It results from this that, in order to have an intense light, one way, at least, would be to have a gaseous substance to burn in order to produce the heat, and some solid particles, or solid substance, to be heated by it, to afford the light.

This is very simple, and yet this is the philosophy of the modes generally adopted to produce artificial light and to increase the intensity of it.

Take a common lamp or candle, for example, burning with a naked flame—that is, without any glass chimney. The tallow, or wax, or spermaceti, or paraffine, or oil, or kerosene, or whatever other similar combustible is used, is composed chiefly of carbon and hydrogen, and all these substances are called, accordingly, *hydrocarbons*. When they are burned in the wick of the candle or lamp, the hydrogen, which is the gas, burns and produces a great heat, and the floating particles of carbon, which, though exceedingly minute—too minute altogether to be seen by the naked eye—are yet solid, become intensely heated, and it is they that emit the bright light.

Hydrogen, burning alone, emits a very feeble light. We sometimes see, in a wood fire, faint blue flames here and there which have very little illuminating power. These are usually flames of hydrogen, and are produced in places where, for some accidental reason, hydrogen only for a few minutes happens to issue. They would be found to be very hot if we had any way of testing their temperature, but they would afford but a very feeble light to write by if by any means we could bring one of them to the table.

The flame of an alcohol lamp is almost entirely a hydrogen flame, and, though it is very hot, it gives very little light, on account of there being no solid particles of carbon in it to be intensely heated by it and to emit their superior light.

It is all the better, on this account, for the purposes that the alcohol lamp is used for—namely, for producing heat; for, if there were solid particles of carbon in the flame, just so far as the force of the heat should be expended in heating them so as to give light, there would be less heat for the water, or the coffee, or the blowpipe, or for any of the other heating purposes for which the flame was used.

And then, besides, the floating particles of carbon in the flame, if intercepted by any substance before they are consumed, blacken it, or, as we say, *smoke it.* If you hold a piece of cold iron or any other such substance in the flame of a candle or lamp, it becomes smoked, as we say. The philosophy of this is, that a great many of the floating particles of carbon are intercepted by the cold substance before they are consumed, and so become attached to it, and blacken it. This proves that the particles of carbon are really in the flame all the time, though we do not see them, nor see any indications of their presence, except in the *increased brightness of the flame,* in consequence of their being themselves heated intensely hot in it and in process of being consumed. But by holding the iron, or any cold substance, in the flame, we at once cool all the particles that come in contact with it, and so stop their combustion, and then their true character is at once revealed.

Very often a portion of the particles of carbon escape from the flame themselves without being burnt, and go up the chimney in the form of a blue smoke. The white vapors which are seen arising sometimes from a fire are vapors of water or steam, but the blue fumes are composed of particles of carbon, some of which escape out of the chimney into the air, while a portion of them lodge upon the sides of it, forming soot.

Some substances give out a much greater quantity of carbon in burning than others, as, for example, birch bark, pitch-pine knots, and the "light-wood," so called, of the Southern States. A great portion of this carbon is made incandescent in the flame, and gives out great light. That is the reason why those substances make such excellent torches. Of the carbon which is thus made incandescent in these flames, some is burned—that is, it finds oxygen enough to combine with it in the flame—and so disappears as carbon, and forms another substance. But some of the particles which are made incandescent—that is, red hot—in the flame, and so help to emit light, are *not* burned, because there is not oxygen enough for all. This portion, then, escapes into the air, where it cools and becomes black again—that is to say, each separate particle becomes black; but generally, when it comes from a common fire, being more or less mingled with a certain portion of watery vapor, which is white, the mixture assumes a bluish hue. When, however, it is not so modified—as, for instance, sometimes when issuing from the smoke-pipe of a steamer —it shows, by its very dark bluish color, what its true character is.

The cause of this escape of carbon unconsumed is that the supply of oxygen for the flame is insufficient; for, whenever a particle of carbon becomes red hot in the *presence of oxygen*, it immediately combines with it, and forms another substance which is entirely invisible. There have been devised in modern times many modes of furnishing supplies of oxygen for flames in a more rapid and abundant manner, so as to prevent the escape of any unconsumed carbon, but in early times no method was known of doing this. Indeed, the necessity or desirableness of doing it was not understood, for scarcely any thing was known before the middle of the last century in regard to the true nature of flame, or of the conditions on which the greater or less degree of light which could be derived from it depended.

Accordingly, in early times lamps were used, quite artistic sometimes in external form, but very rude and imperfect in respect to the principle on which they operated. There was no arrangement to facilitate the supply of oxygen, nor to prevent the disturbing and cooling effect of currents of air upon the flame, so that a faint and flickering light, accompanied by a great deal

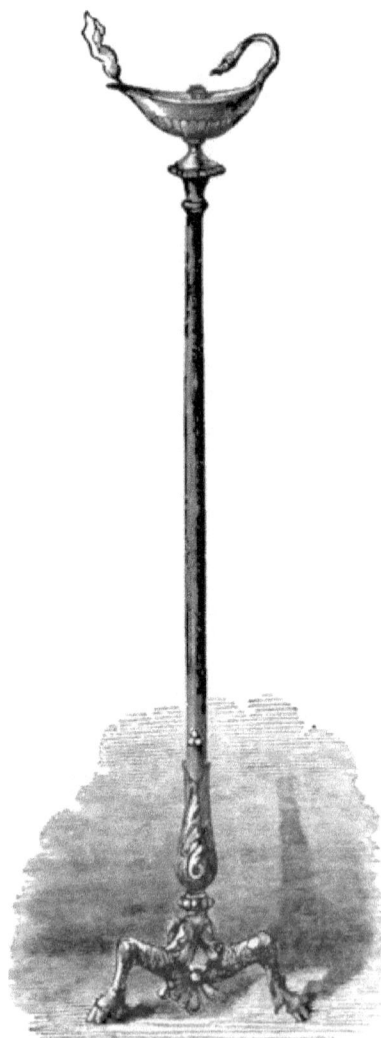

ANCIENT LAMP.

of unconsumed carbon in the form of smoke, was the certain result.

The only light for the streets of cities in Europe two or
three hundred years ago was furnished by great flaming
and smoking torches carried in the hand. The darkness
at night, of course, afforded great facilities for the commis-
sion of all kinds of crime, and robberies, murders, and as-
sassinations increased to such a degree that the government of Paris at one time organized a guard of armed men
to patrol the streets in search of the criminals, lighting their
way, of course, by the only kind of illumination they then
knew how to produce, viz., that of blazing and smoking
torches, which the link-man carried before them in his hand.

The true remedy for this state of things was to dispel
the darkness which occasioned it by devising some way to
increase the brightness of the light which could be given
by a flame, and then lighting the streets by placing a fixed
burner of this increased brightness at every corner.

The first method of attempting to do this was by means
of a reflector placed behind the flame, so as to throw all
that part of the sphere of light issuing from the flame,
which would naturally go back toward the wall, where it
was not wanted, forward into the street. But very soon
the attention of scientific men began to be turned to the
question whether the intensity of the light itself could not
be increased by increasing the intensity of the heat produced, and then promoting the rapidity of the combustion
by a more complete and rapid supply of oxygen. There
would evidently be a double advantage in this, for, by furnishing a full supply of oxygen, all the carbon would be
consumed, instead of being allowed in part to escape unconsumed as smoke, and then, moreover, the particles which
were consumed would be raised to a higher intensity of
heat, and so would become more highly luminous.

THE POLICE OF OLD TIMES.

Now, in the case of an ordinary fire of wood or of coal, the way to increase the supply of oxygen is to blow it with the bellows; that is, to send in, by means of the bellows, a rapid current of air containing the necessary oxygen. But it is a curious circumstance that, while the blowing of a solid fire makes it burn all the brighter, blowing the flame of a candle puts it out. What is the reason of this?

Fully to understand the reason, it must be observed that blowing a fire has three different effects upon it—first, to supply oxygen to it, and so make it burn faster; secondly, to cool it; and, thirdly, by its mechanical impulse, to *blow the burning fuel away*. In the case of the blacksmith's forge, only the first of these effects is produced to any considerable extent. The current of air supplies oxygen to increase the combustion, which greatly increases the heat. It brings coolness too, and so prevents the heat from becoming as great as it would be if the bellows could blow hot air instead of cold; but the influence of the greater supply of oxygen in promoting the combustion is vastly greater in increasing the heat than the cooling effect, even in the coldest winter day, is in diminishing it. And as to the third effect, the coals being solid and comparatively heavy, the current of air is not strong enough to blow them away.

If, however, we imagine that the blast was so powerful as to blow the coals from the forge all over the blacksmith's shop, the fire would be put out by it at once—that is, as soon as the individual coals had time to go out in their new places, scattered over the bench and floor. If the coals were very small, this would be very soon; and if we imagine each one of them to be no larger than a particle of dust, the extinguishment would be almost instantaneous.

This is precisely what happens when we blow out a can-

dle.   The flame is a burning or incandescent gas, with extremely minute particles of solid carbon, infinitely finer
than any visible dust, pervading it.   When you blow it,
therefore, with a strong puff of air, the whole incandescent
gaseous mass is blown away, and is instantly cooled below
the point of combustion; in other words, it goes out.

If there is at the time, however, a portion of the *wick* incandescent, as there usually is, that, as it can not be blown
away, remains burning, and the more you blow upon it the
brighter it glows, until, as fast as successive portions of it
become loosened and driven off, the incandescent mass is
diminished; and as the coolness of the blast prevents the
combustion from extending itself to portions below, the
wick, as well as the flame, is soon entirely extinguished.

So much for the philosophy of blowing out a candle.

CHAPTER VIII.

THE ARGAND BURNER.

In view of the facts and explanations given in the last chapter, it is easy to understand that one way, at least, of attempting to increase the light given out by any flame is to continue some mode of increasing the supply of oxygen for it *without dispersing or scattering the burning materials;* in other words, of "blowing" the candle or fire without blowing it out.

It was a Swiss inventor named Argand who first contrived to do this, and the contrivance which he devised is called the Argand burner to this day.

But, in order that you may clearly understand the principles of his invention, I must first say that there are two ways of "blowing" fires in furnaces and forges: one by *driving in* the current of air by the force of propulsion below, and the other by *drawing* it in, by the force of exhaustion in the chimney above.

The former is effected by means of bellows, and sometimes by another contrivance called a fan-blower, by either of which a strong blast is forced into the fire at the grate. In some furnaces where a very great heat is required, the air is heated before it is driven into the furnace, so that the full effect of the additional supply of oxygen may be secured without any diminution being caused by the coolness of the current of air.

The latter of the modes above mentioned—that is, the drawing of air in by the force of exhaustion in the chimney above, is effected by making the chimney very tall.

The air within the chimney, being heated, is light and buoy-
ant, and, of course, the taller the chimney, the more buoy-
ancy there is, and the greater the draft—that is, the faster
the air is "drawn in," as we usually express it, though the
real mode of operation is that the pressure of the atmosphere above the fire being taken off, in part, by the buoy-
ancy of the hot air in the chimney, the air is *forced in* to
the fire by the atmospheric pressure which acts on the orifice below.

Now Argand's plan was to furnish the increased supply
of oxygen to the fire in the flame of the lamp or candle by
"drawing it in" from below by means of a chimney, and
he also conceived the thought of bringing in the current in
the *middle of the flame* instead of around the outside of it.

Argand, as has already been said, was a Swiss.   He was
of quite humble origin, but he received a scientific education, and in the earlier part of his life he was engaged very
successfully in the southern part of France in connection
with industrial occupations, in which his scientific knowledge, and especially his knowledge of chemistry, were of
great service.

His attention was called, while thus employed, to the
subject of light, especially for use in manufacturing and
other such establishments; for in those days—near the
close of the last century—there was nothing in use for artificial light but such naked, smoking, and flickering flames
as are given out by common lamps, torches, and flambeaux.
His knowledge of chemistry showed him that the reason
why the flames were not bright was the scantiness of the
supply of air, which could only reach the flame on the outside.   It had been discovered some time previously that
an ordinary flame was hollow—being bright only on the
outer surface of it—as, of course, it must be, as in the case
of such a flame there is no access to the air within.

So Argand set himself at work to contrive a way by which to admit air to the centre of the flame; and after a great many experiments and a great deal of contrivance, he succeeded in producing a cylindrical wick which was to be inclosed between two concentric tubes, with an opening at the bottom of the inner tube for a supply of air. He also provided suitable mechanism for raising and lowering the wick, and fitted a sheet-iron chimney over it to increase the draft up through the inner tube.

He made his chimney of sheet-iron, because in those days they had no means of making glass chimneys that would stand so great a heat without breaking. Of course it was necessary to place the chimney so that the lower edge of it should be just above the upper edge of the flame, in order that the light might not be intercepted.

Not long after this the glass-makers contrived to make glass chimneys which would stand great heat provided they were heated gradually, and then Argand's invention was complete.

But the invention, great as its value has proved to be for mankind, was the source to the unhappy inventor of it of nothing but trouble and sorrow. He became involved in disputes and lawsuits with other men, especially with a Frenchman, whose name is spelled Quinquet, and is pronounced, as nearly as can be represented by English symbols, *Kaingkay*. Quinquet, it would seem, drew Argand's idea from him in conversation, or, at least, obtained such glimpses of it as enabled him to produce a lamp of the same character; and he harassed and thwarted Argand in all his attempts to obtain what would correspond to a *patent right* to it at the present day. Argand went to England, and there was more successful. His invention was adopted in that country, and was recognized as his, and the contrivance is called the Argand burner there and in

America to this day.   But in France the name of Quinquet finally carried the day, and a lamp there, with a burner on this principle, is always called a Quinquet.

Argand was worn out, mind and body, by his long-continued disappointments and troubles, and when he was only a little past middle life he returned to the home of his childhood in Switzerland, poor, disheartened, and miserable, and died in the imbecility and wretchedness of a premature old age.

And now, nearly a century since his death, they who understand these facts, after they have been reading for an hour in the evening by the bright light which his simple and beautiful contrivance has given them, sometimes pay a brief tribute to his memory by observing for a moment in silence the brilliant and beautiful effect produced by the double current of air, intensified in its action by the draft of the chimney, and then saying to themselves, "Poor Argand!"

CHAPTER IX.

INTERMINGLING OF UNDULATIONS.

As has already been stated, there are, or, rather, have been, two theories in respect to the physical nature of light—one, that it consists in the emanation of streams of exceedingly minute particles, which fly through the air with inconceivable swiftness, having in some mysterious way the power of passing through glass and all transparent bodies; and the other, that it consists in a vibratory or undulatory motion in a subtle medium, which, in order to have a name for it, has been called *ether*. The existence of this ether is only imaginary, however, as nothing is directly known in respect to it, and it is only supposed to exist, as the sole means that we can conceive of to render the transmission of luminous undulations possible.

It seems, however, as has already been said, very difficult to conceive of the possibility of undulations in such infinite number and variety as must be moving at every point in space, if this theory is true, meeting, and encountering, and crossing each other without in the least degree interfering with or disturbing each other's motions. Still we can not say that this would be impossible. There is complete and positive proof that sound is produced by vibrations in the air; and yet, on a calm summer morning, we can, by listening, hear a great many different sounds, all clear and distinct, and each produced by its own undulations, coming through the same medium with all the rest, and each without being sensibly disturbed by the others. We can hear the songs of two or three different birds, the talk of children at play, the whistle of a distant locomotive, the bark of a dog, the crowing of a cock, the chirp of a cricket, and the faint tones of the bell in the village spire, miles away. Though we can not well *attend* to all these sounds at once, we can hear them all, and, if we select any one to listen to specially, we can hear it distinctly and clearly, showing that the undulations which produce it come to us through the air undisturbed by the undulations of all the rest, which, however, they must necessarily traverse at every conceivable angle on the way.

John had a curious opportunity to observe the phenomenon of undulations crossing each other without serious interference one evening while he was with Lawrence in London. It was in St. James's Park.

There are several large parks in London where people go for recreation and amusement. The nearest, and, in some respects, the most attractive of these, is St. James's Park. This park is smaller than any of the others, but it is nearer the heart of the town, and so is more accessible to large numbers of people. The queen's palace and gardens are near it on one side, the houses of Parliament, and Westminster Abbey, and the Horse Guards (the great headquarters of the army) on another, and the streets all around it are lined with gay shops and elegant residences.

In the park is a long and beautiful lake, crossed in the middle by a suspension bridge. There are walks along the margin of the lake, and chairs for people who wish to sit and rest, and beds and borders of flowers, and swans, and ducks, and other kinds of swimming birds upon the water, and on pleasant summer evenings the grounds are full of ladies, and gentlemen, and children walking about and amusing themselves in various ways.

One evening, about an hour before the sun went down, as Lawrence and John were walking together in one of the

streets in that part of the town, on their way home from
Westminster Abbey, where they had been spending an
hour wandering about through the aisles, and transepts,
and chapels, looking at the monuments and other curious
things to be seen there, Lawrence stopped, and, pointing
to a side street, said,

"I am going to turn off here and go into the park.
There is an experiment that I am going to have performed
there for you."

"Who is going to perform it?" asked John.

"A couple of ducks," said Lawrence, gravely.

John laughed, but he turned very readily in the direction which Lawrence indicated.

They soon entered the park by a ponderous iron gate,
and, after walking a little way over a broad gravel walk
well filled with parties of ladies and gentlemen, and boys
and girls, going to and fro, and separated on each side
from the shrubberies, and lawns, and beds of flowers by an
open iron fence, they came to a suspension bridge leading over a narrow portion of the lake. They crossed
this bridge, and then, after proceeding a little farther,
they found a row of chairs, which were placed by the
side of the walk and facing the water. They took their
seats in two of these chairs, and looked out upon the little
lake.

Immediately before them, across the walk, was a band
of green, with large trees here and there upon it, so near,
however, that their branches intermingled. Under these
trees there was a view of the water, with ducks swimming
here and there over the surface of it. The sheet of water
was not very wide, and beyond it, the farther shore was
covered with groves of trees and thickets of shrubbery.

"Well," said John, as soon as they were seated and had
viewed the landscape before them for a moment, "and

THE DUCKS ON THE LAKE.

what is the experiment that the ducks are going to perform ?"

"It is an experiment on the *crossing of undulations*,"
said Lawrence. "You see these ducks are swimming about
in all directions, and each one, as he parts the water with
his breast and his paddling legs, makes two lines of waves,
or undulations, which diverge from each other as they recede behind him, or, rather, as he advances and leaves
them.   There is something very curious in the laws of
motion that govern the formation and the spread of these
lines; but I am not going to say any thing about that
now, but only to have you see what the effect is when two
of these lines of waves cross each other.   You would think,
in such a case, that they would disturb and destroy each
other, as one would suppose the undulations or vibrations
of light would do.   But you will see, when we get a good
chance—that is, when two ducks happen to come along
side by side, so that the lines of waves cross each other—
that there is much less interference than one would sup-

pose, and that the different lines go on after the crossing much as before."

Just at this time a neatly but plainly dressed woman came along the walk, having a little leathern bag hanging by her side. She advanced to Lawrence, and held out her hand for the money to pay for the chairs.

" How much ?" asked Lawrence.

" Two pence," said the woman—or, rather, as she pronounced it, " tuppence."

Lawrence gave her the money, and she went away.

" I thought they were only a penny apiece," said John.

" That's for the common chairs," said Lawrence. " We have taken arm-chairs, and so have made ourselves first-class people.

" We might as well have taken the common chairs," said John; " they would have been just as good for us to sit here and see the ducks."

" Exactly," said Lawrence; " only then we should have marked ourselves as second-class people. Every thing is managed in England on the principle of social classification. When other people don't class you, you have to class yourself. Americans almost always prefer to pay the difference, rather than make themselves second-class people. But the English don't care so much; they are used to such distinctions."

" *I* don't care much," said John.

" The difference does not amount to much in such a case as this," said Lawrence, " but it is worth thinking of sometimes, as, for instance, on a long journey. When we go to Paris, you can save a pound or two, I suppose—which would be equal to five or ten dollars—by going second class, and so have that amount to spend for apparatus or books in Paris."

" Then I'll do it," said John, jumping up suddenly from

his chair. "I'll certainly do it; I'd as lief go second class as not."

"Very well," said Lawrence. "But now look at the ducks; there are two coming now directly before us in just the right position."

The two ducks that Lawrence referred to were swimming along nearly side by side, at a short distance from the shore, and the little line of waves which passed off from the left side of one crossed that which came from the right side of the other, but the two lines seemed scarcely to interfere with each other at all. They appeared to go on after the crossing, each on its way, as if it had been very little disturbed by the other.

This is only one among the innumerable cases occurring in nature which show the possibility of the coexistence of different vibrations among the same set of particles—that is, in the same substance—with a degree of independence of each other which, without proof from experiment, we should have thought impossible. John was very much surprised to see how little disturbed the diverging lines of waves made by the two ducks were in crossing each other. It is true that afterward, when he saw several ducks swimming this way and that, in all directions, a good deal of irregular commotion was produced on the surface of the water; but this apparent confusion seemed to be caused quite as much by the difficulty of following with the eye, and separating by the mind, all the different lines, as by any actual interference in the undulatory actions.

The case of different sounds coming through the air to the ear, which has already been referred to, is another instance of the coexistence of different vibrations in the same substance, each preserving unimpaired its own distinctive character. So, when a bell is struck—especially if it is a large and heavy bell—besides the general vibration which emits the principal and dominant tone, there are always a great many others which blend with the principal one, and combine with it in the effect of producing the general sound. These subordinate tones are called the harmonics. It is so with a musical string or wire; it has its *harmonics* as well as its principal sound, and they all come together through the air to the ear without interfering with each other. So, when a band of one hundred performers is playing, it is wonderful to think what an immensely complicated mass of vibrations, produced by so many kinds of instruments and playing so many different parts, must come to the ear through the air at the same time; and though many of them may mingle and blend so as to produce a delightful harmony, they do not disturb or derange each other at all, for if they did so the result would be only a discordant noise.

"Such cases as these," said Lawrence, "make it just possible for us to conceive that the emanations of light, moving constantly, as they do, with such amazing velocity, and in every direction through the starry heavens, without interfering with each other at all, *may* be propagated, as scientific men now suppose, by undulations or oscillations in a very subtle and highly elastic medium.

"At any rate," he added, "this much is certain, that these emanations are propagated, in some way most mysterious to us, in *right lines*, diverging in every direction from the centre; that they expand in two dimensions as they advance, and so each portion of them occupies a space that increases as the square of the distance, and, of course, that the intensity on a surface of given magnitude *diminishes* as the square of the distance, or, as the mathematicians say, is *inversely* as the square of the distance; and, finally, that these rays are wholly invisible to us, except so far as they are intercepted in their passage and *reflected*, so as to come to us and enter our eyes, where they form an image on the retina and produce vision."

When Lawrence had said this, he took out his watch, looked at it, and said,

"Well, we have been here looking at the ducks, and talking about the intermingling of vibrations and undulations, about twenty minutes, or twenty-five. Shall we call this time study hours or not?"

"That is just as you say," replied John. "I've *learned something*, at any rate, and something that I did not know before."

"And you have listened attentively to it," replied Lawrence. "I think it would be fair to consider it study hours. And there is one thing more that I should like to explain, which will take about five minutes, if you are not too tired, and that will just make up the half hour."

John said he was not too tired, and would like very well to make up the half hour. So Lawrence explained that, although the emanations of light, whether they were really of the nature of undulations or not, did not appear, in ordinary cases, to interfere with each other at all, however numerous and complicated their intercrossings might be, that still there was an optical phenomenon which was called *interference*, although, strictly speaking, it was not interference in the common sense, since both of the radiations in these cases produced its own full effect, though the two effects combined produced a somewhat remarkable result.

Lawrence explained the principle by asking John to imagine that two ducks were swimming over the water in such directions that the undulations should not cross each other, but should follow each other in long lines exactly parallel.

"Now we may suppose," he added, "that these lines are

more or less near to each other. We may imagine them to coincide exactly—that is, that the crest of the wave of one shall coincide exactly with the crest of the wave of the other, and the hollow with the hollow—and that by this coincidence the height of the wave would be increased, and also the depth of the hollow, so that the two undulations combined should form a united one of double intensity. We can also, on the other hand, imagine that the two sets of undulations may be separated from each other by *half the breadth of the wave*, so that the hollow of one should just correspond with the swell of the other, and thus that each should *counteract the effect of the other*, and the water consequently remain smooth."

"Oh, Lawrence," said John, "it would not be possible to fit the two lines of the waves so exactly as that."

"True," replied Lawrence ; " but is it impossible to conceive of it ?"

"No," rejoined John, "I don't think it is impossible to conceive of it."

"You are right, probably," added Lawrence, "in saying that it would be impossible to perform this experiment with any waves and by means of ducks, but it can be represented perfectly by artificial waves."

" Artificial waves ?" repeated John.

" Yes," replied Lawrence ; " there is an article of apparatus by which the action and appearance of waves can be produced by means of bars of wood rising and falling, so as to illustrate the laws of their motion. You turn a crank, and a motion representing a wave runs along the machine. With this they can show very plainly what I have been explaining to you. There are two sets of moving bars, or two systems, either of which alone makes a line of waves. When they are combined in a way to make the elevations and depressions of both systems *correspond*, the waves are of double height; but when they are combined so as to make the elevations of one correspond with the depressions of the other, then there are no waves at all. The mechanism moves, but the surface of the water, or that which represents the surface of the water, remains smooth."

"That's curious," said John.

"And so with light," added Lawrence. "There is a way of contriving to make the two sets of luminous undulations unite in such a manner as to produce darkness. I can not explain to you now how it is done; only remember that in the books it is called *interference*. It is only interference, however, in one sense. Strictly speaking, neither interferes with or hinders the real and proper action of the other, but the two actions combined produce a remarkable result.

"And now," added Lawrence, rising, "your five minutes are out, and more too, and it is time for us to go home. Only you must try to remember exactly what is meant philosophically by *interference*, as the word is used, in the science of light."

As Lawrence and John walked over the suspension bridge on their return home, they stopped to watch the motions of the ducks and swans which were swimming about in one place near the shore. John looked attentively to see whether he could detect any thing like the phenomenon of interference in the optical sense, but he could not.

"At any rate," said he, "I should like to have one of those wave machines that you described."

"You can buy one, perhaps, when you get to Paris," said Lawrence, "with the money that you save by going second class."

John's father was a very wealthy man, and was perfectly willing to supply his son with all the money that he could judiciously use, and Lawrence had full authority to furnish John with whatever he thought was judicious. But they both had the good sense to know that a boy enjoys any acquisition that he may make much more, and feels a more real and substantial sense of property in it, if he has done something to earn it himself by some kind of effort, or sacrifice, or self-denial. A father who supplies his son freely and thoughtlessly with all the money that he wants acts very unphilosophically. He is as unphilosophical as he would be in thinking that it would do just as well to give his boy money to buy fish of a vendor going by, as to let him take his rod and line and go a fishing himself to catch them.

CHAPTER X.

REFLECTED AND TRANSMITTED LIGHT.

A GREAT many curious and beautiful illusions are produced by the reflection of light. One of the most remarkable of these is the exhibition of pretended ghosts and hobgoblins at places of public entertainment. John went with Lawrence to witness one of these exhibitions at a place of instruction and amusement in London called the Polytechnic Institution, where the whole process was explained. I shall presently give an account of this visit, but in the mean time, in order that the reader may clearly understand the nature of the phenomenon, it is necessary that he should pay attention for a moment to a certain mathematical principle.

If you throw a ball from your hand to the floor *directly* downward—that is, at right angles to the floor, its tendency is to rebound directly upward—that is, to come up as it went down, namely, at right angles.

On the other hand, if you throw the ball somewhat forward, so that it shall strike the floor at some distance before you, it will, in rebounding, go still farther on. In this case the ball strikes the floor at an oblique angle, and, on rebounding, or *being reflected*, as we might say, it rises at the *same angle* on the other side.

It follows from this that if a boy and a girl standing at a little distance apart are playing with a ball, and the boy wishes to throw the ball so that the girl may easily catch it on the rebound, he must throw it so that it shall strike the floor as nearly as possible midway between them, so that it may have a horizontal distance to rise in equal to

that which was occupied in its descent; for this it must
have if it is to rise at the same angle and attain to the
same height.

There is the same tendency, substantially, when the ball
is thrown against a perpendicular wall, though in this case
the effect is modified to a greater extent by the weight of
the ball.

In the case of the reflection of light, the effect has nothing to interfere with it, and the result is, that universally
the angle at which the light comes to the reflecting surface on one side is the same as that at which it leaves it
on the other, or, as it is expressed scientifically,

The angle of incidence is equal to the angle of reflection.

This is one of the fundamental laws of optics.

The principle is made plain by the engraving, where C

ANGLES OF INCIDENCE AND REFLECTION.

represents a small hole in a shutter admitting a ray of light from the sun into a darkened room. The light falls upon a mirror lying horizontally upon a table, making with the perpendicular, A D, the angle of incidence, C D A. The ray is reflected in the direction D B, as far to the right of the perpendicular as it came in on the *left;* in other words, making the angle of reflection, A D B, equal to the angle of incidence, A D C.

An instrument has been devised for showing that these angles are exactly equal, so far as mathematical principle of this kind can be shown by experiment. The next engraving represents this instrument.

It consists of a graduated circle, in the centre of which the mirror is placed, as shown at *n.* Attached to the graduated circle are two slender tubes, A and B, made movable upon the arc. The distance of each from the central point above can be easily determined by the graduation. It is found, in experimenting with this instrument, that when one of the tubes, A, is so adjusted on the arc upon one side, and the instrument is so placed upon the table that a ray of light from the sun passes through the tube to the mirror, and the other tube is placed at the *same distance* on the other side, then, and only then, will the ray, after reflection, pass out through the other tube, B.

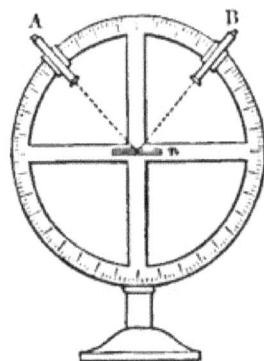

MODE OF MEASUREMENT.

In the same manner, when the two tubes are placed at the same distance from the upper middle point of the arc, no matter what the distance is, a person looking through one of them will see any small object—a key, for example, held at the opening of the other, showing that in all cases the angles of incidence and reflection are equal.

Almost all substances reflect a greater or less portion of the light that falls upon them. When a substance does not reflect light at all, it appears black. When the surface is very smooth—as smooth as it is when we say it is *polished*, and is at the same time *plane*—then it reflects the light regularly and uniformly, and we have an image of the luminous source in it. This is because a sufficient number of the rays are simply turned from their course and directed toward the eye to form vision. They move at the same angle, in relation to each other, after they are reflected as before, and so enter the eye just as they would have done had they not been reflected, but only came from a different direction.

But when, on the other hand, the surface is not polished, then the portions of the surface on which the light falls are broken and irregular; for, even though we call it smooth, it is not perfectly smooth, and the different portions of it reflect the light each in its own way. Thus the light comes to our eyes in a confused manner.

You can get a clear idea of this by first supposing that a looking-glass is lying in the bottom of a basket, whole, so as to reflect clearly and distinctly objects seen in it, and then that afterward it is broken into pieces, and the pieces lie in confusion in the basket, all, however, right side up. The reflections would, in this last case, be confused. You would see a general light, but no distinct image.

This is precisely what happens in the case of ice. When it is whole, and has a smooth and level surface, it reflects the ice like a mirror; but when it is broken up into fine pieces, it presents a general white appearance, like snow, and that is all. Snow itself consists in minute sheets and needles of ice, any one of which, by itself, reflects light like a mirror; but it is too small to reflect any complete object, however minute, and so all the reflections coming con fusedly together to the eye produce the sensation of whiteness.

There is another thing very curious about reflection, which it is necessary to understand, in order that the manner in which the ghost illusion is produced may be fully intelligible. It is this, that the light reflected from any mirror into the eye appears to come from an object lying in the direction of the rays *as they enter the eye.* This must of course be so, for the vision is produced *in the eye,* and by the rays which enter into it, and its character is of course determined entirely by the character of the rays and the direction in which they are moving *when they enter it.* In other words, the impression made upon the eye is determined entirely by the condition of the rays of light after they enter the organ. It can take no cognizance of any changes these rays may have undergone on the way.

This is illustrated in the engraving, where a portion of the light from the candle is reflected from the mirror and enters the eye. But you will see that it enters the eye from such a direction, and with such a degree of convergence—as is shown by the upper arrow—as if it had come from behind the glass. Of course it produces such an image in the eye, and such a conception in the mind, as if it had really come from that position; just as if the glass, instead of being a mirror, had been transparent, and the light had come from an object behind it in the position and in the light necessary to send rays directly to the eye, such as were really sent to it by the reflection.

In the engraving, only that portion of the rays from the candle are represented which comes to the eye. Of course, in fact, the radiance, in such a case, emanates from the flame in every direction, and some portion of it is reflected from every part of the surface of the glass, and is dispersed to almost every part of the room. It follows from this

APPARENT DIRECTION.

that an eye in any place to which the reflected rays come, if turned toward the mirror, would have an image of the candle formed within it by means of a different beam, and, of course, the candle would appear to each observer in a different place behind the mirror, namely, in a place corresponding to the course of his own particular beam.

Thus, if there were twenty persons looking at the reflection of the same candle in the same glass, there would be *twenty images, distinct from each other* in this sense, namely, that each would be seen reflected in a different part of the glass from the other, and would be produced by a different beam of light.

You must remember, then, that the mental perception we have of any object, formed by the image of it in the eye, depends entirely upon the manner in which the light

from it enters the eye, and not at all upon any changes in
direction or in character that it may have undergone before it enters.   This is one of the principles on which illusions are created, namely, by causing the light to enter
the eye in the way it would enter if it came really from
such a source as would correspond with the intended illusion.

There is one other curious thing to be observed in order
to understand clearly the philosophy of the ghost illusion,
and that is, that while opaque substances, such as the metals, will only *reflect* light, without transmitting any—that
is, will throw back what falls upon its surface, but will not
allow any to pass through its substance from the other
side, transparent substances, like glass and water, will *reflect a part* of the light which falls upon them, and allow a
part to *pass through*.   Thus we can look out *through* a
window into the street, and see what is there, and we can
also often see the reflection of the fire, or any other bright
object in the room, on the inside.   When you look out
through a window from a room, and, still more, when you
look into a shop window from the street, it often happens
that you can not-see clearly on account of the "glare."
This glare is only the reflection of light from the glass on
your side of it, which reflection prevents your seeing clearly the *transmitted* light, or, rather, seeing *clearly the objects
on the other side*, which can only be seen by *transmitted
light*.

Thus, when you look into any such glass—that of a window, for instance, some *reflected* and some *transmitted* light
comes to your eye—that is, some light from your face, and
the other objects on the same side of the glass with yourself, which is *reflected*, and some from the objects on the
other side which is *transmitted*, or, in other words, which
passes through: of these two it is the strongest that con-

quers—that is, it is the light from those objects which are most strongly illuminated, on whichever side they may happen to be, that makes the greatest impression on the eye.

Thus the objects in the open air are usually much more brightly lighted than those in the room, and so, in looking out at a window, we see the trees, and the houses, and the people in the street, the light from which is strong, and is transmitted to us *through* the glass, while we do not see the objects in the room reflected in the glass, because the light from them is much feebler; and though it is reflected just the same, notwithstanding that the transmitted light is coming through, it does not affect our vision much in presence of the brighter light that is transmitted.

But if you hold a candle, a lighted match, or any other bright light before a window, you see the reflection of it at once in the pane, even in the daytime. You can also see even a piece of white paper reflected in a window-pane, unless there is a very bright light outside.

So, in the evening, when the room is lighted up, while it is nearly dark outside, the objects in the room are then the best illuminated, and the light reflected from them overpowers altogether, in the effect produced on the retina of the eye, that coming from the street, and it is much more difficult to see any thing outside on account of this reflection. You have to hold your hands up on each side of your face to cut off the light from the objects in the room, which would otherwise be reflected too strongly.

This explains the reason why it is sometimes, especially in a bright day, difficult to see plainly what is in the shop-windows along the street, especially if the panes are of plate-glass. You see the objects in the street by the *reflected light* in the panes, because the light from them is stronger than the light from the objects within.

So, in the daytime, when the light is stronger without

than it is within the room, those in the room can see what
is passing in the street very well, while those in the street
can not see distinctly what is passing in the room. In the
evening, however, the case is reversed. Then, the room
being better lighted than the street, we have always to
close the curtains, for otherwise, the light being greater
now within than without, those who are within can not see
easily the objects without, while those without can see
very plainly what is passing within.

This principle, simple as it is, operates in a thousand different
ways, and intelligent young persons, who once understand
it, will take pleasure in discovering examples of
it which will be continually coming under their observation, if they have only learned "how to observe."

It is often, for example, well illustrated in the case of
water. Water is transparent, and the surface of it, when
left in repose, makes plane and polishes itself, thus forming
a mirror; so that we can see objects on the bottom by
light which comes up through it, or objects on the banks

REFLECTION FROM WATER.

by light which is reflected, which we see most distinctly depends upon what is most brightly illuminated.

When the water is tolerably deep, so that the bottom receives little light, then the reflected light predominates in the eye, and we see, as in the engraving, the buildings, and the trees, and the grass along the shore, and even the forms of the ducks swimming on the surface, by reflected light. The light, too, is reflected in accordance with the principle already explained, namely, so as to make the angle of incidence equal to the angle of reflection. The course of only two rays is given in the engraving—one from each of two points in the eaves of the buildings, to show the principle. In truth, however, there would be an infinite number of rays from each of these points, diverging in every direction, and striking the water at every angle, all of them being reflected on the other side of the perpendicular to each, at the same angle they made in coming to the surface. But only those which fell upon the water at such an angle as to cause them to proceed, after reflection, to the eye of the boy, would take effect in his vision, and he would see the image of the points from which they proceeded in the direction in which they came to him, as shown by the dotted prolongation of the lines beneath the water.

In the same manner, from every other point in the buildings and in the adjoining trees light would be radiated, and would fall upon the water at every angle, and those rays that fell at the right angle to be carried, after reflection, to the boy, would aid in completing the picture of the landscape in his eye. Thus he would have an image of the entire scene upon his retina, the several parts of it appearing as far below the water as the real object was above, except so far as the effect would be modified by the higher or lower portion of his eye.

If the water were *perfectly* smooth, then the image would be perfectly clear and distinct. But this can never be, as the surface of water is never perfectly smooth. It is ruffled by slight movements of the air in the calmest days. In this case, the ripples made by the swimming of the ducks affect it: and even the swimming of fishes or of frogs, far below, is sufficient to produce some change in the surface, and to prevent absolute repose.

When water is deep and the bottom is dark, we see the reflection most clearly, for then there is very little transmitted light coming up through to disturb it; but when the water is shallow, and the objects on the bottom are bright and clear, then we see the reflection indistinctly or not at all, for the reflected rays are overpowered by those which are *transmitted* from below.

These are, then, the fundamental principles on which the ghost illusion depends, namely, that any material which is at once transparent in substance, and also plane and polished upon its surface, like a plate of glass, for example, will *transmit* and also *reflect* light at the same time, so that you can see objects *through it* and objects reflected *in it* together, and the comparative distinctness with which you see them depends upon the comparative intensity of the light with which they are respectively illuminated.

CHAPTER XI.

SPECTRES AND GHOSTS.

ONE of the principal cross streets of London is Regent Street. It crosses the great thoroughfares which run lengthwise through the vast city, and which are the scenes of the principal movement to and fro, being filled in all the business hours of the day with long lines of cabs, and omnibuses, and drays, and coaches, and carriages of all sorts. These long thoroughfares, extending for many miles, are lined with shops of every kind; but Regent Street, which crosses them in the gayest and most fashionable part of the town, is emphatically the street of shops, or *stores* as we call them in America; for the goods, and wares, and objects of interest and curiosity, and the novelties of dress, and articles for presents, and books, and engravings, are more numerous and splendid, and more tastefully arranged behind the great windows of plate-glass here than in any other part of London. If you wish to buy any curious or pretty thing to bring home with you as a souvenir of London, there is not a better place to look for it than Regent Street.

There is one part of the street that is more splendid than the rest. At the lower end of it, where it approaches the region of the houses of Parliament, the club-houses, and the palaces of the old nobility, it makes a grand sweep in the form of a quarter of a circle. This part of the street is known, in fact, as the Quadrant; and as the buildings on each side are uniform in architecture throughout the whole length of it, and as the shops are, if possible, more gay and

E

splendid than those in other parts of the street, the Quadrant is quite a celebrated place for going a shopping in, especially for strangers and visitors in London.

The Polytechnic Institution, or, as it is more commonly called by abbreviation, the Polytechnic, is situated in Regent Street, though it is in the straight part of it, at a considerable distance from the Quadrant. John saw one day an advertisement in the papers of an entertainment that was given there every evening, in which the manner in which ghost illusions are produced on the stage was to be explained, and he felt a strong desire to go and see it.

"Yes," said Lawrence, "I should like to go too; but, so far as the showing of a ghost is concerned, I can do that here myself for you in this very room."

"But you can't do it as they do it at the Polytechnic," said John.

"On the same principle," said Lawrence. "I could not do it on so large a scale, and I could not make the illusion complete, because I could not conceal from you the means by which I should do it; but I should do it in precisely the same way, so far as the optical principles are concerned. Still, I should like very much to see how they do it at the Polytechnic."

"And I should like to see how you do it your way," said John.

"Very well," said Lawrence.

So saying, Lawrence took from the table a card, and cut out from it a figure which formed a rude resemblance to a ghost—that is, a fantastic figure, with its arms extended, and covered with a sheet.

There was a shelf outside the window of the room that Lawrence and John were in, placed there apparently to hold flower-pots, though there were at that time no flower-pots upon it. There were also upon the mantel-piece a number of ornaments, and among the rest an image of a cat, in a sitting posture. Lawrence went to the mantel-piece and took this image from it, and then opened the window and set the image outside upon the edge of the shelf.

"There," said he, "I am going to see if I can't frighten that cat with a ghost."

He then lighted one of the candles by means of a match, and brought it near to the window, holding his ghost in one hand and the candle in the other. He placed John near the window, directing him to look at the cat. Then he held the figure of the ghost a little behind John, and over his head, and also held the candle in such a position that it should shine upon the figure, and yet not shine into John's eyes. The consequence was that a strong light was thrown upon the paper ghost, which made the reflection of it plainly visible near the place where the cat was seen by direct vision. In other words, the light from the image of the cat came *through* the glass from the outside by *transmission*, while that from the ghost, from the inside, on striking the glass, came back to the eye by *reflection*; and thus the two images were produced side by side on the retina of the eye.

"Is that the way they do it?" asked John.

"Yes," said Lawrence, "that is exactly the way in principle, only they do it on a much larger scale, and they contrive to conceal the means. Here, for instance, the ghost, being only a paper card, is lifeless, and the cat is lifeless too; whereas the effect would be the same if they were both alive, and could move, so as to increase the appearance of reality."

"A cat would not do for that," said John, "for cats are not afraid of ghosts."

"How do you know?" asked Lawrence.

"Because, if they were," said John, "they would not dare to go about nights as much as they do."

"They could have a man, then," said Lawrence, "and he could pretend to shoot the ghost, which it would be very safe for him to do, since he would only shoot at nothing— in the air. The real person by which the appearance was produced would be on the other side of the glass, far away."

"He might break the glass, then," said John.

"No," replied Lawrence, "for the image is not *in* the glass, but far *behind* it—as far behind it, in fact, as the real object is before it. The image of my little ghost, for instance, appears, not *on the surface* of the window-pane, but out on the shelf, where the cat is—as far, in fact, from the glass on the outside as I hold the paper from it on the inside."

Here Lawrence moved his card backward and forward, nearer to and farther from the glass, and showed that the image seemed to advance and recede in a manner exactly corresponding to the movement of the object.

Any reader of this book can see how this was done by cutting out such an image and holding it up near the window, with a lamp or candle near, to illuminate it strongly. The effect will be greater if this is done in the evening, before it is quite dark, so that there shall be no bright light shining upon the objects in the street, but only enough to make them visible.

"If I wished to make a representation of the ghost at the other side of the street," continued Lawrence, "then I should have to carry back my paper ghost to the back side of the room, and make it a great deal larger. I might have a real person, with a sheet over his arms, to represent the ghost, so that he might make gestures and walk about, but the principle would be the same in that case as in this.

THE GHOST ILLUSION ON THE STAGE.

But even then the illusion would not be complete, for the real ghost, and the light shining upon him, and also the glass of the window in which he was reflected, would all be seen. In the contrivances for producing these illusions on the stage, all these things are concealed."

So saying, Lawrence took a book out of his trunk and opened to an engraving in which the arrangements usually made for producing such illusions on the stage were represented and fully explained.

You see here a copy of this engraving. The glass is a large piece of plate-glass, like a very large looking-glass without any silvering on the back, and it covers the whole front of the stage. In the engraving the edges of the glass are seen, but in the actual performance these edges are concealed by the curtains coming close to them on each side. Of course the glass must be extremely large. It is placed, too, in an inclined position, so that all the light shining upon it from the side toward the audience is reflected downward, and thus it produces no "glare."

The figure which is to form the image of the ghost in the glass is in front of the stage, and is placed low enough to be entirely concealed from the view of the spectators. It is strongly illuminated by a very bright light, which is also concealed under the stage. The light, of course, radiates in every direction from the figure, and spreads over the whole surface of the glass, whence it is reflected all over the theatre; and a certain portion of it, sufficient to form an image upon the retina, reaches every spectator, and such an image, moreover, as if the light, instead of coming up from beneath the stage, and being reflected by the glass, had really come from an equal distance behind the stage—that is, from the place where the image seems to stand, near the man who is pointing a pistol at it.

This man would, however, not see any image at all near

him, any more than a person behind a looking-glass standing out upon a floor would see the images reflected in it to those before it. The figure is represented there only to show how it would appear to the people in front.

In the same manner, the outline of the figure upon the glass itself is only imaginary, being sketched there only to show how and where the light is reflected. There would be no such image really there. The only things that would actually exist would be the figure below, the light emanating from it, and the images of it in the eyes of the spectator. In other words, what the spectators really see is the figure itself, only they see it by light coming to them in zigzag lines, or, at least, lines taking one sharp turn, as it is reflected in the glass, instead of in direct lines; and as the short turn taken by the rays of light at the glass is altogether outside of the eye, their sense takes no cognizance of it, and the object appears to them as if it were seen directly before them on the stage.

CHAPTER XII.

THE POLYTECHNIC INSTITUTION.

LAWRENCE and John set off one evening about seven o'clock to go to the Polytechnic. They went up through Regent Street, and, as they had plenty of time before them, they stopped along the way to look into the shop-windows, to examine and admire the curious and beautiful things that were to be seen in them. At length they arrived at their destination. The building presented somewhat the appearance of a church. They passed in through the porch in company with many other persons, and stopped on one side, as they went in, at a little office to buy their tickets. The tickets were a shilling—that is, an English shilling—each. The value of an English shilling is about a quarter of a dollar.

When they were fairly within, they found that the interior of the principal room was still more similar, in its arrangements, to a church than the exterior had been, for it was of an oblong shape, with an open floor below, and galleries above all around supported by pillars; only, instead of pews, the floor below was filled with small steam-engines and large articles of apparatus; and the floor of the gallery was also flat, and had a range of curiosities and little machines over the balustrade in front, and upon shelves against the wall behind, with an open space for people to walk in between. Where the pulpit usually is in a church there was a great tank, ten feet square and very deep, which was filled with water, and over it there was hanging an immense diving-bell, ready to go down.

Lawrence and John walked about for some time among these things, observing and examining all that they saw, until at length they came back to what would be called in a church the singers' gallery, where there was a seat, upon which they could sit and rest themselves, and, at the same time, look down over the balustrade to the scene below.

Immediately beneath them, on the lower floor, was a steam-engine, and various other machines connected with it. A little farther on was a large table with a blowpipe, and several other contrivances attached to it for glass-blowing. The glass-blower was sitting at the table at work, making a great many curious things, and a number of persons—young men, young women, and children—were standing around the table watching the operations, and buying the articles which the man made as soon as finished, or selecting them from a large supply of similar articles which he had on the table before him, and which he had previously made.

It was curious, John thought, to see the process of spinning glass silk as this man performed it. He had on his left hand a *wheel*, about a foot in diameter, which was mounted on a stand, and made to turn by a crank. To spin the glass thread, or silk, he held the end of a glass rod in the flame of the blowpipe before him, to keep a portion of it melted, or at least softened enough to be drawn out into a fine thread, and this thread, as fast as it was drawn, he wound round the wheel, turning the wheel all the time with his left hand.

Of course Lawrence and John could not see the thread from the distance at which they were sitting, it was so fine; but they could see the glass rod, and the glow of light at the end of it, where it touched the point of the flame of the blowpipe, and they could also see the wheel turn, which served as a reel to wind the skein upon.

"I should not have thought it would be possible to spin glass in that way," said John, "and certainly not to spin it so even and true. I looked at a piece of it when I was down there, and it was just as even in every part as a hair, and very fine, and yet the man does not seem to take any pains to make it so even."

"It evens itself," said Lawrence. "There are one or two very curious principles involved. There is one that you will think is specially curious, if I can only explain it so that you will understand it. You see that, the hotter the glass is, the weaker it is, because it is more fluid; while the colder it is, the stronger and stiffer it is. Now, in drawing out the glass, it gets cold and strong just in proportion as it gets thin, and that holds it in the thin and slender places, and prevents it getting thinner.

"In other words," continued Lawrence, "just so fast as any parts of the thread get thinner than the rest, they cool at once, and become stronger, and that brings the force to act upon the parts which are thicker, and, of course, more soft, and they are drawn out until they are as thin as the rest."

The same principle operates on a larger scale in pulling candy, and it is by the effect of it that it is so easy to make the candy into sticks so uniform and even.

Just at this moment a bell was rung, and there was an immediate movement among the audience toward a certain door behind the place where Lawrence and John had been sitting. They immediately rose and followed the multitude, supposing that the bell was a summons to hear the lecture on ghosts. There was a great crowding and jamming in getting through the door, each one apparently being eager to obtain a good seat.

Lawrence and John pressed onward with the crowd, and, when they at last entered the room, they found that it was a lecture-room arranged somewhat like a theatre. There was a small stage at the farther side, with a curtain drawn before it. In front of the stage was a narrow area, which was open, and a desk, or small pulpit, with a table by the side of it, for the lecturer, at one end, and something that looked like a large and tall box on wheels at the other end. Immediately back of this open area were the seats for the audience, which rose one above another by a rapid ascent, so that every body could see.

There were various exhibitions and performances during the lecture, which continued for about half an hour. The lecturer was the celebrated Professor Pepper, who is distinguished for his tact and skill in explaining and elucidating philosophical principles, and making every thing clear. He had an assistant with him, and the first thing to be done was to darken the room, and then throw a beam of very strong light from a kind of lantern that the assistant had upon the table across the area—or, rather, along the area from one side of the room to the other—before the spectators. The beam made a round and very bright spot upon the wall, but was not visible on its way through the air, or scarcely visible, because there was nothing there to intercept and reflect it to the eyes of the spectators. For you will recollect that, as has been explained before, light is not visible by itself as it passes through space before us, but only so far as it is intercepted by some substance and turned from its course, and so directed into the eye.

There were, however, some few minute motes and particles of dust floating in the air of the room over the area, which served this purpose of intercepting and reflecting the light in some slight degree, so that the path of the beam through the air was not wholly invisible. The assistant, however, soon brought it very clearly into view by using something which emitted a thick smoke or dust of some kind, and which he beat in the path of the beam of light so as to make it very distinctly and beautifully visible. The professor then held mirrors and lenses of various kinds in the path of the beam, so as to turn the light in various directions, and change the condition of it in various ways, thus causing it sometimes to converge and come to a point, and sometimes to diverge and diffuse itself, in which case it made a very large and bright spot upon the ceiling overhead, or upon any part of the wall on which he caused it to fall. The assistant all the time continued to puff the smoke or dust into the path of light, so as to make its course distinctly visible.

After some farther experiments and illustrations of this kind, the time came for the ghosts. The curtain rose and brought to view a small stage, like that of a theatre, only the front of it was closed by an immense pane of plate-glass, which must have been some ten feet square. This glass was, however, not at all noticed by the audience, for it was inclined forward at such an angle as to throw the reflections of all the light that came from the side toward the audience down toward the floor, and under the front of the stage, so that none except those who were in the secret had any idea that there was any glass there. The edges of it, at the ends, were well concealed by curtains coming up close to it.

The spectators, therefore, did not see either the glass itself, or any thing reflected in it. *Their* reflections were all thrown downward. It is true that if there had been any thing bright down beneath the front of the stage they would have seen the reflection of it coming up to them; but good care had been taken to prevent that by making it dark there. The ghost was there, or, rather, the person who was to represent the ghost, but there was no light yet shining upon him to be reflected by the glass toward the audience, and so the audience saw nothing *in* the glass, but only saw *through* it, and, of course, only saw what was actually upon the stage before them.

Things being thus arranged, all that was necessary was to allow the real person on the stage to talk and act as usual until the time came for the ghosts or hobgoblins to appear, when all at once a very bright light was thrown upon the objects representing these things under the stage, when all the spectators in the seats would see them reflected in the glass; and, as the images of them would appear as far behind the glass as the objects themselves were before it, they would seem to be back upon the stage, among the real actors.

There is one curious difficulty, however, in the management of such an exhibition, and that is, that without some special contrivance to prevent the effect, the position of the mirror, inclined at an angle of forty-five degrees more or less, would have the effect of making the floor on which the personations of ghosts and goblins stood under the front of the stage appear in the glass in a *perpendicular position*—that is, up and down—so that the images in it would appear standing out upon the wall, in an impossible attitude. John had observed in the advertisement of the exhibition in the papers that the ghosts would "dance on walls and ceilings," and he had at first imagined that the being able to make them do so would be the special wonder of the performance, and would require very particular and extraordinary, and even, perhaps, quite complicated optical arrangements, instead of being, as it really is, a very *difficult thing to avoid.*

Any one can see this for himself by means of any looking-glass—a small one will answer the purpose perfectly well. You place this glass on a table before you, first holding it in an upright position. You place any object before

SPECTRES BY A DOUBLE REFLECTION.

it, a small doll, for example. Now, so long as the glass
and the doll are both upright, the image of the doll in the
glass will appear upright, and the table, as reflected in the
glass, will appear *level*, as it is in reality. But the moment
that you begin to tip the glass forward, the reflected portion of the table will begin to rise up, and the reflected
image of the doll will incline forward, and what at first
thought seems singular, the apparent movement of what is
seen in the mirror upward and forward will be *twice as
great* as that of the mirror itself forward and downward;
so that when the mirror is inclined at an angle of forty-
five degrees—that is, half way down to the table—the reflected part of the table will be *perpendicular*, and the doll,
instead of standing upright, will be projected forward, as
if she were standing on a wall.

A very good thing to try this experiment with, especially when older brothers or sisters wish to show it to the
younger children, is an image of a mouse, and then the
mouse will seem, when reflected, as if running up or coming down a wall.

Thus, instead of there being any difficulty in representing the ghosts and goblins as appearing to be on a wall,
the real difficulty is to make them appear to be on a level
floor.

There are various means and contrivances used to accomplish this last purpose, one of which is to have another
glass, to reflect the light a second time, and so bring the
position right.

Another is to have the person representing the ghost, or
the figure, whatever it is, placed horizontally on the floor,
and thus it will appear, when reflected, as if standing back
against the wall. You can obtain a general idea how this
is done by holding the looking-glass in an inclined position
before you on the table, and then placing the doll on its

back on the table, with its feet toward the glass.   The doll will thus appear in an upright position in the glass.

In these experiments which you make with the glass, a common table will be found too low, except for young children whose heads just come up above the level of the upper surface of it; for the head of the spectator ought to be about on a level with the middle of the glass.   A chair placed upon a table—a kitchen table, for example—will bring the glass, perhaps, at about the right height for young persons from twelve to fifteen years of age.

In the exhibition which Lawrence and John witnessed at the Polytechnic there were several different performances, in which quite a number and variety of phantasms were made to appear.   One was the figure of a statue, which had the appearance of standing back against the wall of a painter's studio.   Of course it was produced by some kind of statue in pasteboard, which was lying in a horizontal position beneath the front of the stage.   It could be made to appear and disappear at pleasure by throwing a strong light upon it or shutting the light off.   Then there were figures also—some that represented hobgoblins that ran about upon the wall.   One was in the form of a monstrous fat lizard, with four paws and a long tail, that crawled about in a most mysterious manner as he appeared reflected in the glass.   Of course this animal was really a boy, with an artificial shell or coat to represent an uncouth green monster.

Then there were a number of very pretty and agile little fairies in gorgeous dresses, that danced about in the most fantastic manner, so much so that it was difficult to follow them, and to tell whether they were upon the wall, in the air, or upon the floor.

After the exhibition had been continued for some minutes, and it was time to bring the lecture to a close, Pro-

fessor Pepper caused a small curtain in front of and below
the stage to be lifted up, so that by looking down the spectators could see the objects directly that they had before
seen reflected in the glass above—the pasteboard statue,
the lizard, and the other similar monsters, and, what was
prettier than all, the little fairies, who proved to be young
and agile girls, dressed gayly as dancers. There was a
very bright light shining upon them, and the girls bowed
and smiled, and made salutations to the audience in a
charming manner. A moment afterward the light was
suddenly shut off, the fairies and hobgoblins all vanished
in an instant, the curtain which had concealed them was
dropped, the gas was turned on above so as to brighten up
the whole room, and the performance was over.

CHAPTER XIII.

VERY BRIGHT LIGHTS.

For such performances as those which Lawrence and John witnessed at the Polytechnic, and also for many other purposes, a very bright light is required. There are modes of producing artificial light of such intense brilliancy that you can not look upon it directly with the naked eye for a moment.

But, though we can not look upon the light itself without dazzling the eye, the illumination which it produces when shining upon other objects, though exceedingly bright, is very beautiful to see. Then, moreover, when objects are to be seen by reflection in a glass, there is great advantage in being able to illuminate them by a light so strong that it can not be viewed directly without dazzling the eyes.

Besides this, there are a great many cases in which light is diminished by *diffusion* instead of by reflection, and as the diffusion weakens it, as has already been explained, in the ratio, for similar purposes, of *the squares of corresponding lines*, the light must be very bright indeed at the source, in order that it may be bright enough after diffusion.

The engraving on the opposite page, for example, represents what is called a magic lantern. It consists of a kind of lantern, with an apparatus within it capable of producing an intense light, and also of concentrating this light at a point, from which it afterward diverges in such a manner as to produce an enlarged shadow, or image, of any minute

THE MAGIC LANTERN.

object placed near the focus of the light, and throwing it upon a screen across the room, where many persons can see it together.

The first purpose, however, for which the need of a very bright light was felt by mankind was to increase the range of illumination spread over the sea from the lanterns in light-houses. Light-houses on sea-coasts have been in use from very ancient times. It is true that, before the invention of the mariner's compass, ships were very seldom taken intentionally far out of sight of land. But they were at any time liable to be driven off the coast by sudden storms, or to have shores that were near hidden from view by mists, or fogs, or driving rain; and sometimes their voyage would be protracted by unfavorable winds, so that night would come on before they had entered their destined port.

From the effect of these and other similar causes, lights placed at certain points along frequented coasts were very early used, long before any means were known of producing any light brighter than that afforded by an ordinary fire, or, rather, from such as could be produced by the most combustible natural substances that could be obtained, such as resinous wood, or porous materials saturated with pitch, or bitumen, or oil. These substances were placed sometimes in an iron receptacle called a *cresset*, which was raised upon the summit of a high tower, the system requiring, of course, the constant attendance of a guardian to watch and continually replenish the fire.

The vessel containing the fire was called a cresset, from the word *croisette*, a little cross, the iron-work being often surmounted with a cross, in token of the dependence of the poor mariners, in their exposures to the terrible dangers of the sea, on the special protection of heaven.

ANCIENT LIGHT-HOUSE.

There is one thing which it is very important to observe in respect to the manner in which lights upon a sea-coast aid the mariner in finding his way over the dark waters, and that is, that the object is entirely different from that of light in other cases, as, for instance, those in the street, or in a room. These last are intended to *illuminate the surrounding objects* so that *they* can be seen. In these and in all other ordinary cases, the use of the light is not to make *itself* seen, but to illuminate the objects that it shines upon so that *they* can be seen. But the purpose of the light from a light-house is not to enable the observer to see any thing except itself, but to see itself only for the purpose of enabling him to determine where he is. It does not make visible to him the entrance into the harbor, nor show him the rocks and shoals which he is to avoid, but only to show *itself*, and, by so doing, to *mark a point*, for the purpose simply of making known to the mariner where he is. Being guided in this way only in *determining his position*, he must depend upon his chart, or his own knowledge of the coast lines near, for his guidance into the entrance of his haven.

Thus it happens that, for a beacon on the shore of the sea, there is required, not a diffused, but a highly concentrated light, to show itself to the mariner simply as a star beaming from the midst of surrounding darkness. All that the mariner requires of it is that it should show itself to him. He does not expect that it will reveal to him any of the surrounding objects. These he must have in his memory, or in the mental conceptions which he forms from his chart. The light is only to enable him to place himself properly among them.

There is another thing that is remarkable and is very important to be understood in respect to such a light, and that is, that it is only that portion of it which shines in certain limited directions that is useful for the purpose required—namely, that which goes forward over the sea—and of this only that portion which passes along at a *moderate distance above the surface of the water*. The light from any luminous point radiates naturally, as has already been explained, in every direction, so as to illuminate a complete sphere. A very large portion of this sphere is cut off, of course, by the ground. Half of it would be so cut off if the light was at the surface of the ground and the ground was level; but, as the light is raised above the surface, an amount less than one half, though still a very large portion, is thus intercepted.

Then, moreover, as the light of a light-house is not intended to guide travelers by land, all that would naturally shine on the landward side, if it were allowed to have its own way, would be entirely lost. In the same manner, as it is not intended to shine for the benefit of the birds in the air, all that would go upward would be lost. In a word, it is only that comparatively small portion of the sphere of radiance that extends forward over the surface of the sea, and at a small distance above it—as high as the deck of any vessel—that is of any use for the purpose designed.

Now in ancient times, when these lights consisted simply of blazing fires on the summit of a tower, all except this small portion was lost; but in modern times means have been found to avoid this loss by bending that portion of the rays that would naturally take a wrong direction into the right one—that is, by intercepting all or nearly all those rays which would go back over the land, or down into the ground, or up into the air, and turning them in the direction where their services are required—that is, out over the water. This is done by certain extremely ingenious contrivances, through the effect of which the rays which issue from the source of light are collected on all sides and made to shoot forward over the sea, so that, instead of forming a sphere, the range of illumination takes the form of a flat wheel, or, rather, half a wheel, extending forward over the water, and lying very low.

And inasmuch as we can only see any object when the rays from it enter the eye, we can only see the light from a light-house when we are placed within this range. Thus people on the land behind a light-house would not see the light of it at all, nor would birds in the air. A bird that had alighted on the mast-head of a ship coming in a dark night toward the coast would see the light of the light-house like a very brilliant star in the horizon; but if she should leave her perch and fly a few hundred feet into the air, she would lose sight of it, and she might well wonder what had become of it. The truth would be, that all the light which would naturally have come to that point would have been bent downward near to the surface of the sea, for the benefit of the mariners on the decks of their vessels, leaving the regions of the upper air in darkness, the illumination not being intended for the benefit of the birds.

There is required, of course, a very bright and concentrated light for such purposes as this, in order that the necessary amount of illumination may be brought within such a compass that the apparatus within which it is contained, and the lenses and reflectors required for throwing all the radiation from it out over the sea, may not be of an inconvenient or unmanageable size.

A very bright light is also required for the spectral illusions exhibited on the stage, which have been described in a former chapter; for, as it was there explained, it is only a part of the light that falls upon a glass plate that is reflected from it, and, consequently, any object that is to be seen by reflection must be strongly illuminated.

This is especially the case when, as has already been explained, a double reflection is required to produce the desired effect in the best manner. You will recollect that, by one reflection only, in an *inclined glass*, objects that are perpendicular in reality are made to appear horizontal. To remedy this difficulty, and bring the image into a right position, a second reflection is necessary. When, in order to reflect this, two plates of glass are used, as shown in the last chapter, a specially bright light is required to supply the necessary quantity for the double reflection.

F

You must understand, however, that, as was explained in describing such spectral illusions, nothing of all these arrangements and effects is seen by the spectators in front, except the ultimate image seen in the upper glass, and appearing as if it stood upon the stage. The plates of glass; the course of the rays, from the source of light in the instrument where the man is sitting, through its zigzag course to the eyes of the spectators; the two images, one on the lower and one on the upper glass, as well as the form and position of the glasses themselves, are all shown in the engraving of this double reflection for the purpose of showing what the actual track of the rays through the air is in such a case. But we never really see rays passing thus through the air before us. The eye takes no cognizance of any rays except those which actually enter it, and are concentrated by the lens into an image upon the retina. Thus the spectators, in the case of an illusion like this, would be wholly unconscious of all these movements of the light, and even of the existence of the glasses, although one of them would be full before them. The light would only enter their eyes as it was reflected the last time, which would be exactly as if it came from a figure standing behind the glass upon the stage, and thus the illusion is created.

In other words, the ghost seen is simply the reflection of a real figure in a mirror. In ordinary cases we know that the reflection seen in a mirror is an illusion, for the mirror is silvered on the back so as to allow no light from any thing really behind it to pass through, and thus only the objects that are reflected in it can be seen. We see the frame of it, moreover, so that we know that the mirror is there. But, in the case of these spectres, the plates of glass have no frames, and the edges of them are concealed, and we see, moreover, objects *through* the glass as well as those reflected in it. In ordinary cases, when we see ob jects through a glass, we do not see those reflected in it, because the light shining on the objects beyond that are seen through the glass is usually sufficient to overpower, or nearly overpower, the reflected light; but, by throwing a very strong light upon any object that is to be reflected, we can remedy this, and enable ourselves to see the image of the illuminated object by reflection as plainly as we do those beyond the glass directly, as can be shown in a very simple and conclusive manner by the experiment already explained of holding a piece of paper, with a lamp or candle shining directly upon it, near a pane of glass in the window in the daytime. The paper thus illuminated will be very distinctly seen reflected in the glass. Indeed, white paper emits usually so much light that it can ordinarily be seen faintly reflected in the glass, if it is held near, without any artificial illumination; but the brightness of the image will be greatly increased by the brightness of the light shining upon it.

On the same principle, if you stand near a window, with your back toward it, and hold up a pane of glass, or any small piece of glass, before your eyes, you will see the objects out of doors very plainly reflected in it, especially if it is a bright day. You can also see *through* the glass the objects that are in the room, but the objects outside will be seen too, very distinctly, and the more distinctly in proportion to the brightness of the light which shines upon them.

Thus, when for any reason we wish to see any object distinctly by reflected light in a glass which is not silvered, we require a very bright light to shine upon it, and this is consequently one of the purposes for which a very bright light is required.

On what principle and by what methods these very bright lights are obtained will appear in the next chapters.

CHAPTER XIV.

COMBUSTION OF MAGNESIUM.

ONE day, just before the time for dinner, John came home from a ramble which he had been taking through the streets in London. The table was set for dinner, and Lawrence was reading a newspaper, having comfortably established himself in a large arm-chair near a window.

When Lawrence heard the rap which John gave at the knocker at the door, he said,

"There comes John."

He knew him by his rap.

It is surprising how many different modes there are in use among mankind for communicating ideas and intelligence as substitutes for language. One very striking instance is that of the boatswain's pipe, on board ships at sea, which interested John very much on his voyage across the Atlantic in the steamer. The boatswain, as perhaps the reader knows, is the officer on board a ship who has charge of the sails and rigging; and as the winds and waves are often so boisterous that no human voice could be heard at the distance at which commands often have to be given, the custom has grown up among all European nations of the boatswain's giving his directions to the men by means of a peculiar kind of whistle, called the boatswain's pipe, which makes a very shrill and piercing sound, not loud, but so penetrating that it can be heard in the stormiest times above, or, rather, *through* the sound of the heaviest roaring and thundering of the winds and waves.

John had been quite surprised during the voyage at two

things in respect to the boatswain's pipe: first, at the distinctness with which a sound so slender and thin could be heard amidst the wildest commotion of the elements, and also at the great variety of commands that the boatswain could give with his pipe, by means of variations and modulations in the tone of it, which he made by the motion of his hand over a little hole in a part of the pipe from which the air issued. The number and variety of the orders and directions that he could give by this means constituted quite a language.

In the same way, when he landed in England, John was much interested and amused in observing to how great an extent the knockers on the doors were used as a means of communicating intelligence. A single blow with a knocker is the rap of "tradespeople," as they call them—that is, porters bringing parcels, or messengers from the butchers or grocers, or persons having any thing to sell. A double rap is reserved exclusively for the postman. When that sound is heard every body in the house knows that the letters have come, and the person that attends the door must go at once, so as not to keep so important an official waiting. The two strokes generally come very close together —rat-tat—as quick almost as you could possibly speak those two syllables; but, however rapidly they are given, so long as there are two, every body knows that it is the postman. Then, if it is a gentleman or lady, whether belonging to the house or a visitor, there is quite a prolonged rapping, the strokes being usually quite rapid at first, and more deliberate and emphatic at the end—more or less so according to the rank and importance of the person knocking, thus, Rat-tat-tat-a-tat-tat-tat, *tat!* TAT!

Now, in beating such a tattoo as this with the knocker of the door, no two persons, of course, do it alike, and the length and complicateness of the series of strokes admits of so much variety in the knocks of different persons, without the danger of any of them being confounded with the tradesmen's or postman's knock, that almost every individual comes to have his own peculiar rap, and thus the knocker has a language, as it were, of its own, notifying those who are in the house of the rank and position of the person at the door, and, in case it is any inmate of the family, making it known at once who it is.

And this is how it happened that Lawrence, on hearing the knocker sounded at the door while he was reading his newspaper, said at once, "Here comes John."

All this explanation, however, of the language of the boatswain's whistle at sea, and of the knocker on the doors of English houses, is a digression, and it would be somewhat irrelevant in a scientific treatise on light were it not that a language belonging to this same class, and of substantially the same character in respect to its principles, and of, perhaps, about the same scope as to copiousness and extent, has gradually grown up among the light-houses on sea-coasts, by means of which some simple but very important information can be communicated to ships at sea through variations in the light, as will hereafter be more particularly explained.

John very soon came into the room, and as he entered the door he held up a small object between his thumb and finger.

"See," said he.

Lawrence looked up. John advanced toward him, holding out what had much the appearance of a watch-spring coiled up, except that the color was of a bluish-gray.

"What is it?" asked Lawrence.

"Magnesium," replied John. "It is a yard long when it is uncoiled. I bought it for sixpence."

"That's cheap," said Lawrence.

"Yes," said John; "of course I mean an English sixpence. I saw it in a window, and I went in and bought some of it; I am going to burn it, and make a bright light; of course I am not going to burn it all at once, here; I am only going to burn a small piece—half an inch long, perhaps, just for an experiment, and the rest I'm going to take to America."

Lawrence approved of this arrangement, and it was agreed that they would try the experiment that evening after dinner.

There was some question about the fumes which might arise, but Lawrence said he thought that there would be no fumes, as the product of the combustion of magnesium was simply magnesia, which was a harmless white powder; in other words, a finely comminuted solid. Fumes arose from combustion, he said, only when the products, or some of them, were gaseous, so that they might rise and float in the air.

It is true that sometimes, when the products of the combustion, or the substances set free by it are solid, they are developed in the form of a powder so fine as to be borne upward by the current of hot air, so as to produce the appearance of fumes, and sometimes they mingle with true fumes actually produced. This happens very strikingly in the case of the combustion of wood or coal, in which very fine particles of carbon, detached from the substance of the wood or coal, are carried up among the fumes of carbonic acid gas and the vapor of water, which are really the products of the combustion.

Now combustion, as probably the readers of this book remember, is only the rapid combination of a substance with the element called oxygen, which exists abundantly in the air, and has such an eager affinity for many other substances, especially when they are heated up to a certain point, as to combine with them with great rapidity and violence. In doing this they develop or expend so much force as to produce a great quantity of light and heat, which are considered as only two of the many forms of force. To commence this process of rapid combination with oxygen, a *portion* of the substance must first be heated to the requisite point; but, when it is once commenced, it goes on, the heat developed by the combustion raising the successive portions to the right temperature for continuing the process. This heating a portion of the combustible in order to commence the process is what we call *kindling the fire.* All this has already been explained, and must not be forgotten.

Now, when substances are burned—that is, are delivered over to this eager and fierce seizure of their particles by oxygen, the compounds that are produced are called the products of combustion, and these products, of course, vary very much according to the nature of the substances combined. Sometimes they are gases which rise into the air. Sometimes they are powdered solids. In the case of magnesium, the product is the well-known white powder *magnesia,* which is, in chemical language, the oxide of magnesium, or, as it now is sometimes proposed to call it, magnesium oxide.

John knew all this, so that when Lawrence told him there would be no danger from fumes in burning his magnesium, he was ready to assent to it at once.

"But, then," said Lawrence, "there is sometimes a possibility that some fused portion of the substance to be burned may fall down, and do harm in that way. This happens when the heat produced melts the substance faster than there is oxygen at hand to combine with it. I do not know how this may be with magnesium, and so, in order to make our experiment perfectly safe, we will ask the landlady to lend us an old kitchen plate, and burn our magnesium over that."

This was accordingly done. The landlady, when the table was cleared, brought in a plate. John broke off about an inch in length from the end of his little ribbon of magnesium, and for a handle he used a match, first breaking off the phosphoric end, and then making a little cleft with his pocket knife in the wood, by which means he formed a kind of extemporized forceps to hold the magnesium. When all was ready, Lawrence lighted another match and set the end of the magnesium on fire, while John held it over the plate. It kindled with some difficulty, as if the end of the metal required to be raised to a great heat before the process of combining with the oxygen of the air could begin; but, when it was once begun, it went on with a very intense action, producing a light so vivid and dazzling that it was almost impossible to look at it.

The piece of magnesium which was burnt was very short, and it was, moreover, very narrow and exceedingly thin, so that it was soon expended. John uttered some exclamations of delight while the burning was going on, and when it went out he looked attentively at what was left. It was a white substance of exactly the same form with the little ribbon of magnesium, but, on touching it, it fell to an impalpable powder.

" What white ashes!" said John.

" No," replied Lawrence, "that is not properly ashes at all. The ashes left in burning wood are not *produced* by the combustion, but only *left* by it. The substances which are produced by the combustion in the case of wood go off into the air as gases; the ash is only the incombustible substance that is left behind. But the white powder in this case is *formed by the combustion*—that is, it is composed of the magnesium itself, combined with the oxygen."

" Yes," said John, "I know. It is magnesia."

" It is well enough to call it the ashes in common parlance," continued Lawrence, "on account of its resemblance to the ashes of wood or paper in its apparent origin and in its form, if we only know that it is formed, chemically, in quite a different way."

To have been perfectly precise in his statement, Lawrence might have added that the ash left in the burning of wood is mostly composed of compounds of certain metals with oxygen, formed by some *previous* process analogous to combustion, and left in the ground, whence they were taken up by the rootlets of the plants, and *built*, so to speak, into the wood. But the combustion, if it really was a process of combustion, by which they were originally produced, was not the burning of the wood, but took place long before. In the combustion of the wood they were simply passed over and left, whereas, in case of magnesium, the magnesia which results is *produced at the time*, and by the very process of the burning.

" It did not drop upon the plate after all," said John, looking at the plate, which remained perfectly clean after the experiment.

" No," replied Lawrence; " I was almost sure that it would not. I was very confident that the burning would keep well in advance of any tendency to melting; but, in trying philosophical experiments in a parlor, it is always best to take measures for guarding against even the most improbable contingencies."

CHAPTER XV.

THE MAGNESIUM LAMP.

THE brightness of the light produced in any sense by combustion seems to depend upon two things—first, the intensity of the heat developed by the combustion; and, secondly, upon the presence of *solid particles* to be raised to what is called a white heat by this intensity. Gaseous substances, though the heat may be very great, emit usually a comparatively faint light, as is observed in the case of the flame of hydrogen or of alcohol, which substances in combustion, though the heat produced is very great, give rise chiefly to incandescent *gases*. But in the case of magnesium there is not only a very intense heat, but this heat takes effect upon the solid particles of magnesia as fast as they are produced, and causes them to emit a light of the greatest possible brilliancy.

When any solid is heated in a furnace, we observe that it first begins to emit a reddish-colored light, or, as we say, it becomes red hot. When the heat is raised to a much higher degree, the light that radiates from it becomes brighter and whiter, and we say it is *white hot*. This would seem to be the secret of the very intense light given out by the combustion of magnesium. The combustion produces an extremely high degree of heat, and this takes effect on the solid particles of magnesia as fast as they are produced, raises them to the most intense incandescence, and causes them to emit the very brilliant and dazzling radiation which we see.

This white heat, moreover, is not only different in degree

from the red heat, but it seems to be, in some way, of a different kind—at least it is found capable of producing different effects, and it is in consequence of these peculiar effects that the magnesium can be made very useful for certain philosophical purposes. One would suppose that it would be very difficult to devise a lamp for burning a solid metal in the form of a ribbon of wire, or, indeed, in any other form, but the difficulty has been surmounted in various ways. One of the modes by which this has been accomplished is shown in the engraving. The instrument is called the magnesium lamp.

THE MAGNESIUM LAMP.

The metal is used in the form of a wire, which is wound upon the wheel A, which wheel thus takes the place of the reservoir containing the oil in a common lamp. The wire is drawn off from the wheel slowly by clock-work contained in the box B; within the box it passes between two wheels made of gutta-percha, or fitted with gutta-percha surfaces, which substance holds it with a sufficiently firm grasp to draw it forward between them as the wheels revolve. G is the key by which the clock-work is wound up when it runs down, and at T is the tongue of a little catch by means of which the clock-work may be set going or stopped at pleasure. The wire of magnesium is burned at the end C, which protrudes in front of the concave mirror, being pushed forward by the clock-work as fast as it burns, while the magnesia that results from the combustion falls down into the pan E below. F is a thumb-screw connected with rack-work, by which the mirror can be moved backward or forward as required. The whole can be taken up by the handle, which serves, when the lamp is stationary, as one of the legs.

The magnesium light is used chiefly as a substitute for the light of the sun in photography, especially in cases where the light of the sun is not at command, as, for instance, in caverns, and mines, and other dark places. Its intensity, and certain chemical properties which result from, or, at least, accompany this intensity, fit it to answer these purposes extremely well.

It has been used in this way very successfully in photographing interior views of the great pyramid in Egypt, and in many other similar cases, where none but artificial light could possibly be obtained. It is also sometimes used for engineering and military purposes, such as for illuminating works of construction when it becomes necessary to carry them on at night, and also for showing the position and movements of the enemy in case of nocturnal operations in war. When, for example, the garrison of a besieged city wish to make a sortie at night, if they can send off in advance, or at a little distance from them on one side, an intensely brilliant light, their enterprise is greatly aided, and

that in two ways. The light, while they themselves remain behind it in the shade, shows them the enemy and
the defenses, if there are any, which they are to attack,
very clearly, and at the same time dazzles the eyes of the
enemy, bewilders their vision, and confuses their aim.

In order fully to understand what is to follow, the reader
must not lose sight of the principle on which the magnesium light is produced—namely, by the intense avidity
with which the oxygen of the air seeks to enter into re-
combination with the magnesium, from which it was separated by the use of great force when the metal was prepared, and the consequent heat, which raises the solid particles of magnesia to a dazzling incandescence as fast as
they are formed. Magnesium is never found in its metallic form in nature. It is always found already in combination with oxygen, either in magnesia, which is the simple
oxyde, or in some other form or combination in which it is
already oxydated; and the oxygen with which it is combined clings to it with such tenacity that it requires a very
great chemical force to separate it, so as to produce the
metal in a pure and isolated state.

I mean by a great chemical force a force which, though
really very great, is exercised within such extremely small
limits in respect to distance as to be entirely unapprecia-
ble by the senses. We have an example of a force in some
respects analogous to this in the freezing of water, by
which the particles are forced apart only to an inconceivably minute distance from each other, but yet with so much
force as to lift and displace the heaviest walls if they rest
upon ground that the frost can reach, or to break asunder
the strongest vessels when the freezing water is confined
in them; and so, also, with the force with which the juices
are drawn up in the vessels of plants and trees in the process of vegetation. This force, though inappreciable to our

senses, is sufficient to move the heaviest stones, to lift and tear up pavements, and to push up and sustain the materials of which the branches and leaves of the tree are composed, hundreds of feet into the air.

It is by a force somewhat analogous to these in respect to the minuteness of the limits through which it operates, and the vastness of the power which it exerts within those limits, that the particles of the metallic magnesium are held in combination with those of oxygen in all the substances in which it is found in a state of nature. And so firmly is it held by this force, that, though innumerable experiments were made with the substances in which it was combined, it was a very long time before the existence of the hidden metal in these substances was discovered. The discovery was at length made in 1827. Small portions were separated, and the metal, as a metal, brought to view; but it was not until quite recently that methods were devised by which any great quantities could be produced.

Of course, in these attempts, the substance of the magnesium could be brought into its metallic form only by separating the oxygen from it, and this could be done only by applying a greater force to the oxygen than that by which it was united with the magnesium. This force was, as has already been said, very great. Indeed, the eagerness with which it returns to the combination, and which is the cause of the great development of heat and light, is the measure of this force. Thus the chemist, in separating the magnesium from its oxygen in its natural combinations, forces the substances apart for the sake of witnessing the effects produced by the violence with which they come together again. The operation is very analogous to that of lifting a stone high into the air in order to observe the force of the concussion with which it strikes the ground in falling.

CHAPTER XVI.

INCANDESCENCE.

There are various methods by which an intense white light is produced by artificial means, but most of them, if not all, depend on the same principle as that already explained in the case of the magnesium light—that is, in raising particles of a solid substance to incandescence. The two essentials are, first, some method of producing an intense heat; and, secondly, the presence of some solid substance to receive the heat and to emit the light developed by it; for light, for some mysterious reason, is emitted much more powerfully from a solid substance, however minutely subdivided, than from a gas.

The same general principle, indeed, is seen to operate in the case of light derived from the lower, as well as in that from the higher temperatures produced by combustion. This is shown quite clearly in the flame of a common lamp or candle.

The materials used for burning in lamps and candles, as the reader will recollect, usually belong to a class of substances called *hydrocarbons*. They are so called because they are chiefly composed of hydrogen and carbon. Their burning is, of course, the combination of these substances with the oxygen of the surrounding atmosphere.

Now hydrogen, in combining with oxygen, produces, under favorable circumstances, a very intense heat, and forms by the combination the vapor of water. This vapor rises from the flame and is diffused through the atmosphere. We do not see it as it arises, but we can show it very plainly by holding a cold iron over the flame, at a little distance above it, when we shall find it will be almost immediately covered by a dew formed by the condensation of the vapor into a film of exceedingly minute drops of liquid water.

And so, when you light a lamp in cold weather, the glass chimney, if put on cold, becomes for a moment bedimmed with a dew produced by the condensation of the aqueous vapor formed by the combustion of the hydrogen. As soon as the glass becomes warm the vapor is no longer condensed, though it continues to be formed as before.

WATER FROM FIRE.

This phenomenon may be shown in a still more perfect manner by burning a candle for a few minutes under a cold bell glass, and observing the deposition of the water on the interior of the glass, which will sometimes be so abundant as to cause drops to trickle down the sides.

This experiment of condensing water from the products of flame, which any one can easily perform, will succeed better if the iron, or other condensing substance, has some thickness, so as not to become warmed itself too soon, and so cease to condense the vapor; and if it has also a polished surface, as such a surface, by its brightness being dimmed, will show the presence of very small quantities of vapor.

Sometimes children, when they are writing a letter, and are in haste for the writing to dry, hold it at a distance over the flame of a lamp, not knowing that the hydrogen, which forms a large part of the oil, produces water by its combination with oxygen in the burning, and that this water, in the form of vapor, rises directly to the place where they are holding their writing to dry! In other words, they hold their paper in a very damp, though in a very hot place, as is shown at once by holding there a cold chisel, or hatchet, or large carving-knife, or any other piece of polished and cold iron.

The other substance contained in the hydrocarbon burned in the lamp or candle is *carbon*. This, so far as it is really burned—that is, so far as it finds oxygen to unite with it, forms a suffocating gas, called carbonic acid gas, which it is very injurious to breathe. This gas rises with the vapor of water into the air, and is diffused in the upper part of the room till it gets cold, when it descends and gradually escapes through open doors, or windows, or up the chimney. If there is no way of escape for it open, or if there are many lamps, or candles, or gas jets burning in the room, the air becomes gradually so charged with it as to be uncomfortable and unhealthy to breathe.

But all the carbon does not at once find oxygen enough at hand to combine with it. A portion of it remains for a moment in the flame, where it serves the purpose of furnishing a supply of solid particles to emit light. They can not all burn at once, because there is not oxygen enough for all; so that, while some are burning, and evolving great heat in so doing, the others, while waiting their turn to be supplied with oxygen, as if not willing to be idle and useless even for a moment, employ themselves in producing and emitting light, which the heat that is supplied to them empowers them to do. At length, however, when they reach the upper and outer margin of the flame, they too obtain their supply of oxygen from the air, and, combining with it, give out more heat, and also form more carbonic acid gas, which arises with the rest into the air.

Thus, on their way through the flame, after being liberated from their previous combination with hydrogen in the hydrocarbon, and before their turn comes to be supplied with oxygen to enable them to form a new combination, they serve as solid particles, to emit light by their incandescence.

It is from these solid particles—individually solid, though inconceivably minute—that the chief portion of the light of such a flame comes. The combustion of the hydrogen alone, or of any other gaseous substance, though it would produce great heat, would afford very little light. For some mysterious reason, it is necessary that there should be solid particles present to transform, as it were, a portion of the heat into light, and emit it in that form.

These solid particles of carbon in the flame are not directly visible, but, as in the case of vapor of water, we can easily, by the use of proper means, bring them into view. If, instead of holding the cold iron in the air above the flame, we hold it, or any other solid substance, actually in the flame, the black particles are suddenly cooled by it, and deposited upon its surface as soot is upon the back of the chimney. This black substance, on account of its being produced in this way, is called *lamp-black.*

The process which thus takes place in the burning of a candle is quite a complicated, and a very curious one, and if, in watching it, our powers of vision were sufficiently acute to enable us to distinguish the several steps, we should be greatly interested in observing it. In the first place, we should distinguish in the oil, slowly coming up the wick, particles of carbon and hydrogen conjoined. We must not, however, conceive of the particles of carbon as black; they are black when separated from their combinations and existing in a certain form by themselves, but they may be of any other color. Color, as will be explained more fully in a future chapter, depends altogether upon the manner in which any substance absorbs or reflects the light, and this does not depend upon its intrinsic character at all, but apparently upon the mechanical arrangement of its particles. Thus sugar, which is white in the lump, when dissolved in water and diffused through it, loses its whiteness entirely and has no color at all.

The particles of carbon which, combined with the hydrogen, form the oil, have only the *color of the oil* while in this combination. When they come up to the flame, the action of the heat, in some mysterious way not at all understood, has the effect of developing in them a strong tendency to separate from each other, and to enter severally into combination with the oxygen of the air which is near. In combining with the oxygen, we should see them seize it with great avidity and violence, and the force which they thus expend we should see taking the form of heat, which would act upon the next portion of oil which came up, and produce the same effect upon the carbon and hydrogen in that; and thus the process would go on.

The hydrogen which was thus separated from the oil, we should see, would seize upon the oxygen with the greatest avidity, and procure the largest share, or, at least, the earliest. The carbon particles would have to wait, it would seem, for their supply until the hydrogen was satisfied. The consequence of this is, as we should see, that while the hydrogen combines at once with the portion which it requires, thus becoming transformed into the *vapor of water*, the carbon particles, or, at least, a very large portion of them, pass up through the flame intensely heated, and, by the superior power of a solid to radiate light, become the source of nearly all the light which the flame affords.

All this we should see if we had senses acute enough to perceive what really takes place in the burning of a lamp or candle.

The particles of carbon which pass up thus through the flame, though while so hot they emit the yellow color of the flame, in other words, are themselves of a yellow color, become intensely black if they are interrupted on the way, and suddenly cooled before they find oxygen to combine themselves with. They are, moreover, so inconceivably minute, that when assembled together they form an impalpable powder, far softer and finer in the minuteness of the division than it would be possible to make masses of carbon by any artificial process of pulverization. This mode, accordingly, of procuring a black powder for paint, and for painter's work, is practically employed to a great extent. The engraving shows how lamp-black is manufactured on a large scale.

The fire is made in the little grate at *a ;* it is made of pitch, or tar, or some other hydrocarbon containing a large proportion of carbon. The substance is heated by a fire below it, and then is set on fire above, and is furnished with a limited supply of oxygen through small holes made for the purpose. In consequence of this limited supply of oxygen, the combustion is imperfect, and a large portion of the carbon escapes in the

MANUFACTURE OF LAMP-BLACK.

form of a dense black smoke into the chamber *b c,* where it attaches itself to the walls, and also to the sides of the cone *d,* which is placed there to receive it, and can be raised or lowered at pleasure by the cord and pulley. When a sufficient quantity of the deposit has accumulated, it is removed from the walls and the cone, and packed in papers for transportation and sale.

This being the philosophy of the light produced by a flame of a lamp—that is, by the incandescence of solid parts heated by the combustion and floating up through it—it is plain that the way to increase the light is to increase the rapidity of the combustion, so as to increase the heat and raise the solid particles to a higher degree of incandescence. And to increase the combustion, the proper means is to increase the supply of oxygen. The most obvious way of doing this is to facilitate the access of air, since air affords the most abundant natural supply of oxygen that we have at command.

It was this idea which Argand carried into practical effect in his celebrated burner, by which he supplied a current of air on the inside as well as the outside of the flame, and also at the same time increased the rapidity of the supply by creating a draft by means of a transparent chimney, as has already been fully explained.

The same effect in principle is produced in a common form of burner for gas, called the "bat's wing." This con-

THE BAT'S WING.

sists in so forming the opening for the issue of the gas as to throw the flame into a broad, flat form, so as to give the air access to a very enlarged surface of it.

This method, like that of Argand, as well as a great

many other contrivances which act on the same principle, consists obviously in increasing the supply of oxygen by facilitating the access of common air to the combustible substances in the flame.   But common air contains but a small portion of oxygen—one fifth only of its volume; the remainder consists of other gases, which not only render no aid to the combustion, but positively impede it by occupying the space and keeping back the oxygen from approach.   The remedy for this difficulty would obviously be supplying the flame with pure oxygen instead of a mixture containing four fifths of useless matter.   This is done in an arrangement which has been quite celebrated, and which is known as the Bude Light.   This light will, however, be more particularly referred to in the next chapter.

CHAPTER XVII.

FOLKESTONE.

WHEN the time arrived for crossing the Channel into France, Lawrence said to John, on the morning of the day before, that he had a bargain to propose to him.

"Good!" said John; "I agree to it beforehand."

"You know," continued Lawrence, "that there are four or five different routes of travel from London to Paris, crossing the Channel at different points. Now the bargain which I have to propose is, that you shall choose the route for us to take, without my having any thing to say about it, on two conditions."

"Very well," said John; "let us hear the conditions."

"The first is," said Lawrence, "that you are not to decide blindly. You are to 'study up' the subject, as they say in the guide-books, and find out what are the relative advantages and disadvantages of the different routes."

"I agree to that," said John.

"And the second is," continued Lawrence, "that you are to take the whole charge of both of us on the passage. I am to have nothing to do but to be quiet and do as you say."

"And how about the money?" asked John.

"Of course," said Lawrence, "I am to put you in funds before you set out."

John was much pleased with this proposition, and was ready to agree to it at once. After a very careful and thorough research in the guide-books, he decided upon the route through Folkestone and Boulogne.

This is one of the two routes which take you across the Channel in the narrowest part, thus giving a smaller portion of the journey to be made by steamer on the sea than the other routes which cross the Channel lower down, where it is wider. The other passage leading across the narrow part of the Channel is from Dover to Calais. This last was far the most usual route in ancient times, when steam-boats were unknown, and the passage was, accordingly, always made by sailing vessels, which did not pretend to leave port at fixed hours, but only when wind and tide favored.

Now, of these two routes, the passage by Dover and Calais is the most romantic in two respects—first, on account of the quaint and antique character of the two towns, and the many very interesting historical associations connected with them; and, secondly, from the fact that, as the boat by that route leaves every day at a fixed hour, whatever is the state of the tide, and as the water in the harbor there, as in most of the other harbors on the shores of the Channel, is never very deep, and is nearly all out at low tide, it happens that, when the tide is low at the appointed hour of sailing, the steamer necessarily goes out of the harbor some time before, and remains outside, in deep water, until the hour arrives, and then the passengers go out in a small boat to go on board.

John thought it would be a very interesting adventure for him to go on board in this way in a small boat, and for that reason was inclined to take the Dover route.

But then he did not know, and he had no ready means of ascertaining, whether the tide would be low or not at the time of sailing on the following day; and if it should not be, he saw that he should lose his desired adventure, and would have to go on board in the tame and commonplace way of walking over a plank from the pier.

The arrangements of the Dover and Calais line are made with special reference to the carrying of the mails, which, in order that the postal service between London and Paris may be regular, have to leave at the same hour every day, whatever may be the state of the tide.

But the communication by Folkestone and Boulogne is conducted more particularly with a view to the convenience of passengers. Accordingly, the time of the leaving of the boat from Folkestone is governed by the state of the tide, so that the passengers can always embark on the English side, and disembark on the French side, directly from the pier. This makes it necessary that the hour of departure should change from day to day, according to the state of the tide; and John found, on looking at the time-table, that the hour of sailing for the next day was at ten o'clock in the evening. Now he thought that going on board a steamer at ten o'clock in the evening, and making the voyage in the night, would be more romantic than even going out to join a steamer lying in the open roadstead in an open boat, and so he decided at once in favor of Folkestone and Boulogne.

He rose early the next morning, so as to accomplish one of his three hours of study before breakfast. He would like to have done more than that, but he had not time, and after breakfast he was so much occupied in making arrangements for commencing the journey that he could do no more before setting out. He determined on taking the first train after breakfast.

"You see, by that plan," he said to Lawrence, "we shall have more time at Folkestone; only I should have liked to stay here a little longer, to do some more of my studying."

"You can do it just as well at Folkestone," said Lawrence. "There is an excellent place to write and study there."

"What sort of a place?" asked John.

"The reading-room at the hotel near the pier," said Lawrence. "There is a charming reading-room there, with a very large round table in the centre covered with magazines and pictorial papers, and pretty desks and comfortable arm-chairs at the windows all around the room. There is also quite a large library of books, in a handsome case, on one side."

"That will be just the place for me to study my other two hours," said John.

This reading-room, which is really a very attractive room—more so than any other room of the kind that I have seen in any hotel in England—is a very appropriate and desirable part of the accommodations of a hotel at a sea-port, where people are liable to be weather-bound, so as to have to spend some hours, and perhaps days, in waiting for a storm to abate or for a heavy sea to go down.

Lawrence and John arrived at Folkestone about morning. The town is situated in a kind of dell, opening between the cliffs of the coast. This dell was probably formed in the course of ages by a stream of water, the mouth of which has been deepened and enlarged in modern times, and inclosed in long piers extending out from the land so as to make a harbor. Near the pier on one side is a level plateau, which is laid out in ornamental grounds, in the centre of which stands the hotel, which is called the Pavilion, and which is arranged specially for the accommodation of the travelers departing or arriving by the steamers.

The first thing that John did on his arrival, after giving the porter instructions about the baggage, or the *luggage*, as they always call it in England, was to walk a little about the house and grounds to gratify his curiosity by examining the locality. The main building of the hotel is in the centre, and is used for sitting-rooms and bedrooms, with an office for the reception of guests at the farther end of it. The principal restaurant is in another building facing this; the entrance to this restaurant is under a piazza. In the end of this same building, toward the right, is situated the reading-room which Lawrence had described, and on the left is the regular dining-room. The pier and dock, where the steam-boats lie, is upon the other side of the street from the hotel.

John explored all these precincts with much interest and attention. Among other things, he saw a placard put up signifying that there was a public dinner given every day, or, as they call it, a *table d'hôte*, toward the latter part of the afternoon, where those of the guests of the hotel who liked to do so could dine together. There was also the restaurant, where those who chose could dine at small tables by themselves at any hour of the day.

John went to report these facts to Lawrence, whom he had left in the reading-room, where he was engaged at one of the desks near a window making some memoranda in his journal. But he found that there were a number of ladies and gentlemen engaged in reading and writing in different parts of the room, and he perceived at once that conversation, except in the lowest whisper, would be improper in such a place; so he amused himself in looking at some of the pictorial papers on the table until Lawrence had finished his work, and then they went out together.

John first conducted Lawrence to the placard which contained the notice about the dinner, and asked him what he should do.

"Shall we dine at the public table," he asked, "or have a dinner by ourselves?"

"That is for you to say," replied Lawrence; "I have nothing to do with it. You are taking me from London

to Paris, and all the arrangements of the journey are under your direction."

"Then," said John, "I shall decide to have dinner at the
public table, so that I can see the people."

"All right," said Lawrence.

"Only," continued John, "I do not know whether I can
wait so long. The dinner is not till six o'clock."

"That's bad," said Lawrence.

"Let's have something for luncheon!" exclaimed John,
his countenance suddenly brightening up as if a sudden
thought had struck him.

"I think that is what I should do," said Lawrence, speaking in a somewhat indifferent tone, as if the affair was no
concern of his. "I think, if I had charge of persons on the
passage from London to Paris, I should not expect to let
them go from nine o'clock till six without giving them
something to eat."

"We'll have a nice luncheon," said John, speaking in an
exulting tone. "We will have it in an hour from this
time. I am going to study my second hour now, at once,
before I go out to see any thing ; then we will have luncheon, and after that I am going out to take a walk and see
the town ; then, after dinner, I shall have time for another
half hour of study—from half past seven to eight ; and if
you will give me a lecture of half an hour on board the
steamer while we are going across, I shall be all right."

Lawrence seemed to approve of this plan—at least so
John thought, and it was accordingly adopted. John went
into the reading-room and established himself at the pleas-
antest looking desk which he saw unoccupied, and prose-
cuted his work diligently for an hour, while Lawrence sat
in a very comfortable arm-chair near the great table, and
became apparently much interested in reading some of the
reviews. At the end of the hour they went together into

the restaurant, where they had an excellent luncheon. After the luncheon they set out for a walk. John was full of curiosity to see the pier and the harbor, and also the town and its environs, and the pleasure which he enjoyed in the excursion was greatly heightened by the thought that so large a portion of his work was done.

"I thought at first," said he, "that I would go and take the walk first, and afterward have my hour's study; but I concluded that I should enjoy the walk more to have my second hour of study off my mind."

"That is very good philosophy, I think," said Lawrence.

"I think it was a good plan," replied John, "but I don't see much philosophy in it."

"The philosophy is this," replied Lawrence, "that if you take your study hour first, you have only the work itself to do, and the enjoyment of the ramble afterward is without alloy; whereas if you postpone it, you have the work to do in the end just the same, and the irksomeness of thinking of it and dreading it all the time that you are taking your walk, in addition. Thus you have a double burden in the latter case, and only a single one in the former. So you see there is sound philosophy in keeping well ahead with your work. Duty first, and pleasure afterward, is an excellent rule in respect to the philosophy of it, as well as on other accounts."

The two boys, or the two young men, whichever you think is the most appropriate mode of designating them, enjoyed their walk very highly. They went first out to the pier which formed the inclosure of the harbor on the side toward the hotel. They saw a great number of steamers and of sailing vessels lying in the harbor, most of them aground in the mud, for it was at this time low tide. At the outer portion of the pier was a pretty esplanade, with seats at various places, and a light-house near the end.

There was a great drawbridge over one of the openings into the harbor, made for the passage of railway trains to a great station on the pier opposite the steamer landing. After examining all these things our travelers went into the town, and thence up a long ascending road—with flights of stone steps branching off from it here and there—which led up to the cliffs on one side, where they found long rows of handsome houses, the summer residences of fashionable people from London. There were lawns and other ornamental grounds in front of these houses, between them and the road; and between the road and the margin of the cliff was an open space, serving as a promenade. There were seats here and there, with children playing around them, while those who had charge of the children were sitting upon the seats, sewing or knitting. In other places ladies and gentlemen were walking to and fro, enjoying the magnificent prospect which was spread before them over the sea.

This handsome esplanade, with the sea on one side far below, and long rows of elegant houses on the other, extended a long distance—a mile or more—along the cliffs. In one place John went near enough to the brink of the cliffs to look over. He saw, at a great distance below, a road running along close to the margin of the water, with people walking upon it, and here and there a cart going along. The road looked very narrow, and the men and the carts very small.

After continuing their walk until their curiosity in respect to this place was fully satisfied, Lawrence and John returned to the town in the valley by another way, on the farther side of the range of houses facing the sea.

They reached the hotel an hour before time for dinner, so they took another walk around the harbor, examining the structure of the piers, and looking at the different steamers and vessels. The tide was coming in, and some of the smaller vessels were afloat. They found the steamer there in which they were to go that evening. They knew it by the smoke which was issuing from the chimney, which showed they were "firing up" on board, so as to have the steam ready when the hour should arrive. They went on board this steamer, descending by a long and steep gang-plank, and John chose the place where he said that he and Lawrence would sit during the passage.

When the time arrived for dinner, they went to the ho-tel, which was very near, and after dinner John went into the reading-room, and spent half an hour at his studies. This left him half an hour more of work to complete his task for the day, and this he was going to take, as has al-ready been stated, in the form of a conversational lecture on the passage.

Clouds had begun to gather in the sky before Lawrence and John went in to dinner, and when John had finished his study he found that the sky was entirely overcast, and that it was beginning to rain.

"Lawrence," said John, after going to the door and look-ing out, "it is beginning to rain. There's a storm coming on."

"Yes," said Lawrence, "so I see."

"And what shall we do about going?"

"Do just what you think best," said Lawrence; "you are in command."

"But I can ask advice, I suppose," said John. "What would you advise me to do?"

"Well," said Lawrence, "it is just as you please; but if you ask my advice, I should not advise you to go unless the boat goes."

"Nonsense, Lawrence!" said John. "Of course we can not possibly go unless the boat goes."

"Not very well," said Lawrence. "You might, I suppose, hire a sail-boat."

Lawrence said this with a perfectly grave face, as if he thought that the idea of chartering a small sloop or schooner for crossing the Channel by themselves, on a night and in a storm in which the officers of a steamer thought it not safe to go out, was one to be seriously entertained.

"No; but seriously," said John, "what would you really do if you were I?"

"I don't know what I should do if I were you," said Lawrence, "but in such cases—unless I have ladies under my charge—*my* rule is, if the boat goes, I go, and not without."

"Then *I'll* go," said John.

Accordingly, about half past nine, John conducted Lawrence on board in the rain.

G 3

CHAPTER XVIII.

THE CHANNEL AT NIGHT.

IT was dark on the pier, except so far as the lamps upon the lamp-posts enlightened the scene. There were very few passengers, for travelers crossing the Channel on tours of pleasure—which class of persons generally constitute the majority on board these steamers—usually avoid choosing their time for crossing when the tide serves at night, and some on this occasion, who had intended to go, were deterred by the prospect of a dark and rainy passage, and concluded to remain quietly in the comfortable hotel till the next day.

It was wet upon deck, and so Lawrence and John went below. There they found a small cabin, with tables in the middle of it, and seats along the sides. They chose a place in a snug corner, where they sat for a while amusing themselves with watching the coming and going of the people. One man came in seeming very much out of humor, and uttering very impatient expressions about the weather; and then, after putting down his valise and his parcels, and looking about with an angry air, he stalked out again.

"He is grumbling about the weather," said John.

"Yes," said Lawrence; "he does not seem to be aware that complaining of the weather is complaining of the providence of God."

"I don't think that the weather is more the providence of God than any thing else," said John. "It is all according to the laws of nature."

John had read this in some book, and it is no doubt correct.

"True," replied Lawrence. "The weather is no more controlled by the providence of God than every thing else; and so, when a man grumbles and complains about *any thing* that he can not help, he is repining against the providence of God, and he punishes himself in doing it."

"How so?" asked John.

"He makes himself uncomfortable in getting angry, and does not help the trouble by it."

"But sometimes he *can* help it," replied John.

"I said things that he could not help," rejoined Lawrence. "If there is any thing that he *can* help, he ought to help it."

Just then the engine began to move, and John said the steamer was going to start, and that he must go up on deck to see her sail out of the harbor. In about ten minutes he came back.

"It does not rain any more," he said, "but it is very wet on deck, and the light-house behind us on the pier looks very brilliant. I'm glad we came."

"It is generally best to go if the boat goes," said Lawrence; "that is, if you are a man."

"I'm not a man," said John.

"Or if you are old enough to have much manliness about you," added Lawrence.

"I'm going up again," said John, after a moment's pause.

So he left Lawrence, who was at this time sitting quietly at a table reading. He was gone about fifteen minutes, and when he came back he said that the light-house on the French coast was in view. "It looks like a faint star," he said, "low in the horizon."

"Then the clouds must have lifted, and the air must have become quite clear below," replied Lawrence, "for very rare drops of rain, or even a very little dimness, extending for twenty miles, would entirely intercept the light. Each drop or each vesicle would intercept and absorb a part, and, in encountering the immense number that would be contained in a space of twenty miles, the whole would be expended."

Lawrence then said that he had a plan to propose about John's studies for the next day.

"To-morrow will be rather a hard day for you," he said, "in respect to your three hours' study. You will be up late to-night, and so will not be much inclined to rise early in the morning. Then we are going to Paris to-morrow, and the journey by rail will take up a large part of the day. Finally, the excitement of arriving in Paris, and getting established in a new and strange hotel, will make it hard for you to sit down to study then."

"But I mean to do it, nevertheless," said John.

"You can give it up for to-morrow, you know, if you please," continued Lawrence; "there is no penalty—only you lose a little credit."

"That is just what I don't wish to do," said John.

"Or you can take it for one of your days of failure," added Lawrence. "You are entitled to one day in each fortnight."

"No," said John; "I am not going to have any days of failure, if I can possibly help it. I have not had any yet."

"Then I'll tell you what I propose," said Lawrence. "I will give you a lecture on the philosophy of bright lights now, while we are making the passage; then you can write an abstract or recapitulation of it when we get on shore. Time passes quicker when we are writing than in any other kind of study. My giving you a lecture of half an hour will finish your study for to-day; then, if you choose, after we reach Boulogne, you can begin to write your recapitulation and do half an hour of to-morrow's study to-night; then you can do another half hour's to-morrow morning after breakfast, before we set out for Paris; then one hour of study on the journey, and another of writing, perhaps, after you get to Paris, will make up your time."

John agreed to this proposal, and then they both went to a corner of the cabin, where they could sit together and talk by themselves, and Lawrence commenced his lecture at once.

"The first thing that you are to put down in your reca-pitulation," said Lawrence, "is that the general principle on which bright artificial lights are produced is by raising solid substances of some kind to an intense degree of in-candescence by means of extreme heat. The heat is gen-erally produced by combustion, though not always so. But, however the heat may be produced, it is always by its effect on the particles of a solid substance in causing them to emit a very vivid light that almost all bright lights are made.

"Then, the second thing that you must say," continued Lawrence, "is that, in order to produce the required inten-sity of heat by ordinary combustion, the thing to be done is to increase the supply of oxygen. This is effected, as you know, in the case of the Argand burner, by making the wick circular, and bringing a current of air up on the inside of it, and also increasing the strength of the current on the outside by means of a glass chimney.

"So, after stating the two principles, namely, first, that the light is produced by making solid particles intensely incandescent by means of extreme heat, and, secondly, that, when this heat is to be produced by combustion, it is done by increasing in some way the supply of oxygen, then you can enumerate the five principal modes of producing bright light, and make them subordinate heads in your article,

INTERNAL SUPPLY OF AIR.

and proceed to explain them in order, as I will now go on
to explain them to you.

"The five principal kinds of bright light produced by
artificial means are,

"1. The Argand burner.

"2. The Bude Light.

"3. The Oxyhydrogen Light.

"4. The Magnesium Light.

"5. The Electric Light.

"1. THE ARGAND BURNER.   This I have already explained," continued Lawrence.   "The solid made luminous

by heat consists of particles of carbon, heated by the combustion chiefly of hydrogen from the oil, and increased in . intensity by currents of air both on the inside and outside of the flame.

"2. The Bude Light is the same, except that, instead of currents of air, *currents of pure oxygen* are made to flow in contact with the flame. Air contains only about one fifth of its bulk of oxygen; the rest is nitrogen, which, for the purposes of combustion, is only in the way. The rapidity and intensity of the combustion is greatly increased by supplying *pure oxygen* to the fire. In the burning of magnesium, it is found, by careful comparison, that the intensity of the light is doubled when it is supplied with pure oxygen. In the same way, the light in the Argand burner is vastly increased when pure oxygen is supplied to it instead of common air.

"The Bude light has been used a great deal, sometimes for light-houses, and sometimes for other purposes; but there was found to be this inconvenience about it, that it required the apparatus for producing the oxygen always at hand; and the process required a good deal of attention, and involved some increased expense.

"3. The Oxyhydrogen Light. In the case of the Argand and Bude lights, the solid substance rendered incandescent is composed of particles of carbon, which are furnished, together with the hydrogen for producing the heat, by the oil or other hydrocarbon that is burned. But in the oxyhydrogen light, the hydrogen, as well as the oxygen, is furnished pure, and the heat which is produced by their combustion is directed against the point of a cone formed of *lime*, or some other substance capable of sustaining such a heat without melting or burning, and this lime is the solid substance which becomes incandescent and emits the light."

"The heat produced by the burning in this case—that is, the chemical union of pure hydrogen and oxygen, is *inconceivably intense*. There is scarcely any substance so refractory as to endure it. Any substance, however, that can sustain it, is raised to such an intense incandescence by the heat that it emits a light of the most wonderful power. It has been seen, it is said, at the distance of more than one hundred miles in the daytime.

"The light produced thus by an oxyhydrogen flame projected upon lime is sometimes called, from the source of it, the oxyhydrogen light, and sometimes the *lime* or *calcium* light, and sometimes the *Drummond light*, from the name of the man who first discovered it, or, at least, who first introduced it.

"There is one curious circumstance in connection with this subject," continued Lawrence, "which you can mention in your recapitulation or not, just as you think best, after you learn what it is, and that is, that it makes apparently no difference what the solid substance is which is raised to this intense incandescence in the various methods adopted of heating them. The particles of carbon in the Bude light, for example, are black when they are cold, but they give out a none the less intense light on that account when they are heated up to the requisite point. Indeed, it is very curious that all solid substances, however different they may be in chemical or mechanical properties, begin to become luminous at the same temperature, and are, so far as I know, equally brilliant at the highest temperatures. The reason, therefore, for using lime is not because it is white, but because it will stand the heat without melting.

"But you must remember that while all solid substances become incandescent at the same temperature, and emit, as I suppose, the same quantity of light in comparison with

each other at all temperatures, there is a vast difference in
this respect between solids and gases. Gases, however
highly they are heated, for some mysterious reason or
other, *emit comparatively very little light.* There is a curious experiment to show this. If a thin plate of platinum
is held over the flame of a lamp at a place where the ascending gases are not at all luminous, it becomes incandescent itself at once—that is, a degree of heat which makes
the solid emit a bright light, will not cause the gas to emit
any at all."

" Would it be the same with a thin piece of iron or
steel," asked John—"a piece of watch-spring, for example?"

"I don't know," replied Lawrence. "Perhaps it might
over an Argand lamp, or any lamp on that principle, with
a glass chimney."

"I mean to try it some day," said John.

"I would do so," said Lawrence. "And now for the
fourth light, which is

" 4. THE MAGNESIUM LIGHT."

But what Lawrence said on this head need not be repeated, as the manner in which a very bright light is produced by the combustion of magnesium, and by the intense
incandescence of the solid particles of magnesia which result, has already been fully explained.

"And now," continued Lawrence, after having finished
what he had to say under the fourth head, "we come to

" 5. THE ELECTRIC LIGHT.

"This light is on the same principle with the others in
respect to its being produced through the incandescence
of solid particles by intense heat, and the particles, too, are
particles of carbon; but the heat is produced in another
way, and that is not by any process of combustion, but by
electricity.

"But I think," said Lawrence, "that I have given you a long enough lecture for this time, so I will leave the electric light for to-morrow, when we are going on in the train to Paris."

"Yes," replied John, "that will be better; you have told me now as much as I can well remember. I think I had better make a memorandum with my pencil of the three first kinds of light, and that will help me in writing my article."

So John took his note-book from his pocket and went to the table to make his memorandum.

The time occupied by the lecture was more than half an hour, as a great many things were said which are not recorded in my report of the conversation. Accordingly, when John, after completing his memorandum, went up on deck, he found that the light which was beaming from the harbor at Boulogne was a great deal brighter and seemed much nearer. Indeed, they were now about half across the Channel. They arrived about midnight, and John, finding, when they reached the hotel, that he was too tired and sleepy to write, concluded to go to bed, without attempting to do any of the next day's work that night, which Lawrence thought was a very wise conclusion.

After he had gone to bed, and just as he was going to sleep, he called out through the open door to Lawrence, who was in the next room,

"Lawrence, I forgot all about my plan of going to Paris second class!"

"Never mind," said Lawrence; "lie down and go to sleep."

CHAPTER XIX.

THE ELECTRIC LIGHT.

THE four very bright lights which can be produced by artificial means are, as Lawrence enumerated them in his explanations to John (if we leave out the Argand burner, which is, after all, only the form of a burner, and not a special mode of producing light), the Bude Light, the Magnesium Light, the Oxyhydrogen Light, and the Electric Light. The last named—the Electric Light—is in some respects the most remarkable of all.

The electric light is like the others which have been described in this respect, namely, that it acts on the general principle of *raising solid particles to an intense degree of incandescence by means of extreme heat*, while it differs from them all in the manner in which the heat is produced. In the other three the heat is produced directly by the process of combustion, which, as we have already seen, is another name for the force which is developed by the combination of the combustible—chiefly hydrogen— with oxygen. In this, on the other hand, the heat is produced by a current of electricity, though it is a remarkable instance of the analogy which runs through the operations of nature, that the current of electricity which develops the heat is often produced by the combustion of zinc, or, rather, by a process which is, in a chemical sense, essentially combustion. The current, nevertheless, may be, and now often is, produced in other ways.

In whatever way the movement of electricity is occasioned, it often produces luminous effects. The lightning in the clouds is the most striking of these effects that is witnessed in nature. The aurora borealis is another of the forms in which electrical light is manifested. In certain states of the atmosphere, also, pencils of light are seen upon pointed objects, such as the tips of the masts and spars of a vessel at sea, and the summits of spires and other projecting points of buildings on land.

There is a good deal of mystery about some of the forms in which the light produced by electricity appears, but in that which is developed by artificial means for purposes of illumination, it is well ascertained that the effect is due to the incandescence of solid particles by the agency of intense heat. It is found that, when an interruption is made in an electrical circuit, heat is developed, provided that the current is powerful enough to force its way across the interval. Sometimes the interruption consists of a wire or other conductor too slender to convey the whole current. In this case the wire is at once heated more or less intensely, according to the force of the current in relation to the slenderness of the wire.

This is the way, in fact, in which blasting charges, for example, are often fired in rocks or under water. The cartridge containing the charge is prepared beforehand by two wires coming in on opposite sides of it, and connected together in the middle of the gunpowder by a *very slender wire*, too fine to convey readily the whole electrical charge which is to pass through the circuit. The outer ends of the two side wires are then connected with the electrical battery in such a manner that the charge may at any moment be sent through them. The battery, of course, may be placed at any distance, provided that wires can be laid, or other electrical communications made from the two poles of it to the place where the cartridge is deposited. Then, when the battery is set in operation, and the connections

ELECTRIFIED POINTS.

CHARCOAL POINTS—MAGNIFIED.

are properly joined, the fine wire within the cartridge is instantaneously ignited, and the gunpowder or other explosive material is fired.

When the interruption in the circuit is made under certain circumstances and in a certain way, the intervening space is filled with extremely minute particles, which are detached from the solid substance at one side of the interval and driven across to the other side in a state of intense heat and incandescence. This especially takes place when the two terminations on each side of the interval are formed of *cones of carbon.* In this case particles of the carbon, so minute as to be individually entirely invisible, become detached from one side and pass across through the air to the other in a state of incandescence so intense as to furnish a light which surpasses almost every other artificial light in brilliancy.

And this is the famous electrical light.

The charcoal points used are actually very small. The engraving, however, shows the effect which is produced, and the result of it in modifying the forms of the points, as seen greatly magnified. The globules of melted matter which appear attached to the cones come from the fusion of the earthy impurities in the carbon.

Although the light is thus derived from incandescent particles of carbon, it is not at all due to heat produced by *the combustion of them,* as is, in a great measure, the case with the light which comes from a common fire—that is to say, the heat which renders them incandescent is not the heat derived from *their own combination with oxygen,* but from that developed by the electricity alone, which is vastly more intense than any heat which their combustion would produce. The evidence of this is that the electric light is equally vivid in a vessel exhausted of air, as shown in the engraving on the following page.

H

Above and below we see the two wires conducting the electric current, and connected respectively with the charcoal points within the egg-shaped glass. This glass is closed above around the metallic rod passing down through the cap of it. There is an opening in the upper end of this rod, into which the wire from the battery can be inserted and secured by the thumb-screw, which, however, is so small in the engraving as to be scarcely visible. There is a similar connection below with the other battery wire.

IN A VACUUM.

There is an opening through the stem and the base of the instrument below, by means of which the air may be exhausted—the instrument being placed upon the plate of an air-pump for this purpose—and then the opening can be closed by means of the stop-cock, the thumb-piece of which is seen in its proper place on the left-hand side of the stem.

With this instrument it is shown that the vividness of the light is not diminished by the absence of air, and, consequently, that the source of the heat, by which the particles of carbon are made incandescent, is not combustion, but some mysterious property of the current of electricity to manifest itself under certain circumstances in that form.

All these things about the different modes of illumination, as used in light-houses, and a great deal more about the application and use of them, Lawrence explained to John in the lecture which he gave him in the railway carriage, on their way to Paris, on the day after they crossed the Channel, as described in the last chapter. The lecture was in two parts, of half an hour each, with an interval of two or three stations between. During this interval the train stopped at Amiens for the passengers to take dinner. John had worked for an hour at the hotel at Boulogne before going to the station, and he intended to spend an hour in writing an abstract of Lawrence's lecture when he should arrive in Paris; this would make his three hours' study for that day.

"If I had known all this about the different kinds of light for light-houses before," said John, after the lecture was concluded, "I should have changed my plan about going to Paris to-day."

"What should you have done?" asked Lawrence.

"Instead of going to Paris, I should have gone down the coast of France, bordering on the Channel, to see the light-houses. We are in the best place to see light-houses in the whole world."

"Yes," said Lawrence; "the English Channel is admirably well lighted, on both the French and English sides."

"There are light-houses on every point of land and at the entrance of every little harbor," said John; "I saw a map of them. I suppose there must be a great many different kinds that we might have seen if I had only thought of it."

"It would not have done any good for you to have thought of it," said Lawrence, "for you have no authority to decide that we would go to see them."

"Why not?" asked John. "I'm commander of this expedition."

"Yes," rejoined Lawrence, "but with limited powers; you are in command for the purpose of conducting the party to Paris. You have a right to decide upon any course and any mode of traveling which you honestly think best adapted to take us to Paris in an agreeable and comfortable manner, but you have no authority to deviate entirely from the object for which you were appointed, and take us somewhere else.

"Every body that is intrusted with power," continued Lawrence, "is bound always to keep in mind the object, and the limits of it. For example, if the Secretary of the Navy, who has command of all the government ships, were to fit out a squadron to convey a party of his private friends on an excursion of pleasure up the Mediterranean, he would entirely transgress the limits of his authority. His power over the navy is given to him for a certain express purpose, namely, to serve the interests of the nation in carrying into effect the policy and the measures determined upon by Congress, and his authority is bounded strictly by these limits. If he were to attempt to use the navy for any other purpose or in any other way, he would be impeached and turned out of office. There is special provision made for such cases by the government."

"How?" asked John.

"If any public officer transgresses the limits of his power," said Lawrence, "the House of Representatives bring the accusation against him, and the Senate try him. If he is proved guilty, he is summarily ejected from office."

"But there isn't any government in our case," said John.

"Yes," rejoined Lawrence, "I'm the government—that is, I am the supreme authority in all this tour; and if you had decided to turn off from the route to Paris to go down the Channel in order to visit the light-houses, I should have impeached you and turned you out of office forthwith."

John laughed aloud at this idea, and said that he almost wished that he had done it for the sake of the fun of being impeached and turned out of office.

"Besides," continued Lawrence, smiling a little, in sympathy with John's amusement, "you want to know a good deal more about lights and light-houses yet before you can

visit them profitably. It is always best to know something about the nature and character of any contrivance
before you go to examine it. If we understand the general
plan of a machine, for example, and the principles on which
it operates, before we see it, we can then examine it intelli-
gently. Things have a significance to our minds in that
case which would be otherwise wholly unmeaning. But if
we go to look, for example, at the arrangements and contrivances at a first-class light-house, without knowing any
thing about the principles which govern the operation, we
can only stare at them in bewilderment and wonder, and
go away nearly as ignorant as we came."

John was convinced that this was true, and he determined that on his arrival in Paris he would first write a
pretty full abstract of what Lawrence had taught him in
his lecture, and then he would procure a book about light-
houses, and learn all that he could in regard to the different systems adopted, and the manner in which the arrangements are carried out, especially those relating to light-
houses along the coast of the English Channel.

"And then," said Lawrence, "when we set out on our
return from Paris, if you propose that we should go down
from Boulogne on the French side, visiting the principal
light-houses on the way, and, when we get to Havre, cross
over and come up to Folkestone on the English side, I
shall think it an excellent plan."

On the arrival of the train at Paris, John was greatly excited at the spectacle presented to his mind in the life and
movement of the great city, for this journey was before the
desolation and ruin brought upon it by the great Prussian
war. They took a cab, and went directly to the Grand
Hotel. From the windows of the cab John observed, with
great interest and much excitement, the wonderful sights
presented to his view.

When they arrived at the hotel, and had gone through the preliminary ceremony of entering their names and engaging lodgings, they were shown to their rooms, and there the first thing that John did was to draw up a table near a window and take out his writing materials.

"The first thing that I am going to do," said he, "is to get my hour of study off my mind, then I can go out and see the city entirely at my ease."

This he did. While he was thus engaged, Lawrence went down and waited for him in the splendid reading-room below. The reading-room was much larger and more magnificent, but not so cosy and snug as the one at Folkestone. At the end of the hour John came down, and he and Lawrence went out into the grand court-yard, and thence by an elegant passage, with a roadway in the middle, and a sidewalk separated from the roadway by columns on each side, into the street. John almost leaped for joy at the sight of the scene of gayety and splendor which here met his eye.

"Lawrence," said he, "I'm glad my study is done, and I think your rule of 'duty first and pleasure afterward' is excellent philosophy."

CHAPTER XX.

THE CORRELATION OF FORCE.

THE work of establishing a light-house upon the sea-coast for the guidance of mariners naturally divides itself into two portions, or, rather, there are two distinct ends to be secured, each of which is essential to success. The first is to devise some method of making a *very bright light*, and the second the means of gathering the beams that would naturally radiate backward over the land, or upward into the sky, and throwing them all *forward over the sea*, so that they may be brought to combine their luminous effect in the direction where the light is required.

In respect to the former point—that is, the source of light itself—there are many things to be considered besides the actual brightness of it. The concentration of the radiant point is very important, inasmuch as light issuing from a point is much more manageable by lenses and reflectors than that which comes from a large surface, which is, in effect, the same thing as coming from a great many different points at a greater or less distance from each other. In former times a *compound* Argand burner was generally employed, and is still in very extensive use. This kind of burner consists of several concentric wicks—that is, circular wicks one within another—the outer one being three or four inches in diameter. Such a light, of course, consists of quite a large flame, and is not so easy to be controlled by reflectors or by lenses as the same amount of light from a single point would be; so that when, at length, the means of producing very bright lights from a single radiant point—or at least from a surface of very limited extent, such as the oxyhydrogen and the electric light—were discovered, it was at once seen that some very great advantages would result from employing these methods in light-houses.

But there are other things to be considered besides the concentration and brilliancy of the light employed for this purpose. The facility of managing it, and the absolute certainty of it—that is, its entire exemption from all danger of getting out of order, with the care and attention that a guardian of average skill and fidelity can be relied upon to bestow—are points of essential importance. It is not enough, therefore, that a scientific operator in his laboratory can produce, by ingenious contrivances, a very powerful and concentrated light, and one which he can perfectly manage and control in a lecture-room for the amusement and instruction of an audience. Before his plan can be adopted by a Light-house Board they must know how his light is produced, what would be the cost of it on a great scale, and whether the apparatus necessary for producing it can be managed *safely* and *certainly* by unscientific, though careful and faithful men; and, more than all, whether there is any possibility that, even so seldom as once in five or ten years, the process of producing it might fail, through some unexpected derangement of the apparatus or other accident, so as to leave the mariners who might be on the lookout for it without its warning of their approach to the land for several hours, and perhaps for a whole night. There are, at the present time, about six hundred lights on the English coasts, and if the system was such that a light was liable to be out of order even *once in ten years*, that would make the number *sixty* upon the average that would fail during *some night of every year*. Such an uncertainty as this would greatly impair the confidence of the mariners, and vastly increase the perils of navigation.

The public authorities are, therefore, very cautious about introducing new modes of producing light, especially such as depend upon any chemical process. Of course the oxy-hydrogen light requires the preparation of both oxygen and hydrogen, and the electric light that of a current of electricity. The former renders necessary a chemical pro-cess involving the maintenance of a somewhat complicated apparatus, and a certain degree of scientific supervision in the management of it. These constitute insuperable ob-jections to it in respect to a vast majority of the situations in which lights are required.

These situations are sometimes quite isolated, light-houses being not unfrequently built on rocks at some dis-

LIGHT-HOUSE ON A ROOK.

II 2

tance from the shore, where, in heavy weather, the sea breaks over them with so much force that sometimes for days, and even weeks, the keepers are cut off from all communication with the land. In such cases it is very plain that the modes of producing and managing the light must be of a very simple character. The apparatus must be very little subject to accidents or derangement, and only to such as can be easily remedied, when they do occur, by persons of ordinary skill.

The production of a current of electricity for the electric light was at first, and for a long time, effected by a chemical process involving a considerable degree of scientific knowledge and skill in those directing it, if not in its ordinary and successful working, at least in the emergencies which in all such operations will sometimes occur.

Within a somewhat recent period, however, a method has been devised of developing the requisite current of electricity by means of mechanical force through the medium of magnetism. It is found that changes in the magnetic condition of an iron bar, for example, induce electrical movements in any conductors placed at right angles near it. If an iron bar is wound round with a wire in a certain way, and the magnetic state of the bar, while thus wound, is made to change—which may be easily done by alternately bringing it near and drawing it away from a permanent steel magnet — a succession of electrical impulses are induced in the wire. By combining many of these wound bars—or *bobbins*, as they are sometimes called —in one machine, and causing a number of permanent magnets to revolve in face of them in rapid succession, and then combining the electrical impulses that are induced in a proper manner, the effects, substantially, of a continued flow are secured, so far, at least, as is essential for producing the electric light.

MAGNETO-ELECTRIC MACHINE.

The general principle of this instrument will be seen illustrated in the engraving. It is called a magneto-electric machine, as it is one for developing electricity by means of magnetism. Apparatus which operates on the converse principle—that is, of developing magnetism from electricity, is called electro-magnetic.

The bobbins—that is, the bars of soft iron wound with conducting wires—are in the centre, in a great measure out of view, being arranged around the axis of the machine. This axis may be rapidly revolved by means of the band and pulleys seen above, which bring in mechanical force—provided either by steam or horse power—from the adjoining room. The ends of the bars within the bobbins pass, as they revolve, across the face of the poles of the powerful horseshoe magnets which are seen arranged in tiers on the outside. There are eight ranges of these magnets, with seven in a range. The magnetic condition of the iron bars is changed, of course, with amazing rapidity when the axis is made to revolve at considerable speed. At each change an impulse of electrical force is imparted to the wires around the bobbins. These impulses are combined by means of the proper connections, and thus become practically a continued stream, which passes to and is returned from the carbon points in the instrument on the left. The small square box above the pedestal contains the apparatus for regulating the distance of the carbon points from each other, this being necessary to secure steadiness and uniformity in the light.

The whole process, as exemplified in this apparatus, furnishes a very remarkable and very comprehensive illustration of a principle which is one of the greatest, if not the very greatest scientific discovery of modern times, namely, that of the correlation of force. The principle is, that all the great forces of nature—mechanical motion, electricity, magnetism, heat, and light, are *modes of action fundamentally the same*, in this sense, namely, that they are equivalent to each other in certain definite proportions, and are continually interchanging one into the other, in these precise proportions, in many of the operations of nature around us, and in artificial processes instituted by man.

In the case of this magneto-electric machine we have an example of all these forces transforming themselves one into another, and that again into a third, till in this single process, taking it from the beginning to the end, we run through the whole round.

To bring in the whole of the circuit, however, we must begin with the sun; the *heat*, or other radiation comprised in his beams, is transformed in the leaves of the growing plant into a *latent force*, or "potential energy," as it is sometimes termed, which is stored in the grain or hay eaten by the horse, if we suppose the machine to be driven by horse power, or in the wood which formed the coal, if we suppose it carried by steam. This energy comes out into action in the animal, developing itself as *muscular* force. In moving the limbs of the animal and turning the machinery, the muscular force becomes converted into *mechanical motion*, which is conveyed by the pulleys and bands to the magneto-electric axis. There this force is expended in overcoming magnetic resistance, and is transformed by this action into *magnetic force* in the soft iron bars, and, as it disappears in this form, it reappears as *electric force* in the environing wires. From these it passes by the conducting wires to the charcoal points where it is first transformed into *heat* to make incandescent the solid particles of carbon, and is then transformed into *light*, to radiate over the surface of the sea. The whole process constitutes a very complete and striking example of the correlation, or reciprocal relation of the various forms of force.

` CHAPTER XXI.

FRESNEL.

THE most important object to be sought, after determining the most satisfactory method of creating a bright light for light-house purposes, is, as has already been said, to devise the best means of utilizing it when created by concentrating it in the direction where it is required.

In former times this was done by reflectors alone, the light being placed in the focus of what is called a *parabolic* reflector, which is a reflector of such a form that it reflects the light radiating from the focus within in a beam of *parallel rays* issuing through the opening in front.

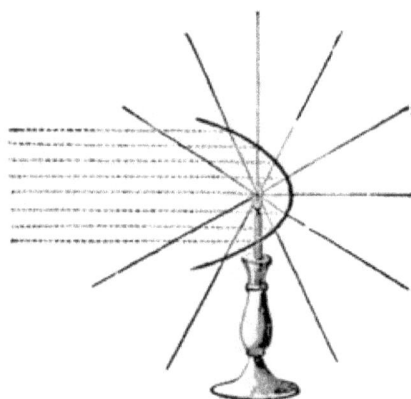

PARABOLIC REFLECTOR.

This is shown clearly in the engraving, the black lines representing the natural course of the rays, and the dotted ones the lines into which they are turned by the reflector and formed into a parallel beam.

We see this arrangement in operation in the front of the

railway locomotive at night, making the light far more effectual on the track ahead than if a simple lamp without a reflector, however bright it may be, were used.

For we must remember that light, in radiating from the luminous point through the atmosphere, loses brilliancy as the distance increases, from two causes; first, from the spreading or diffusion of it, on account of the divergence of the rays from each other as they recede, which causes the intensity of it to diminish, as we saw in a former chapter, *as the squares of the distances;* and, secondly, on account of the interception of the light by solid or liquid particles always floating in the atmosphere, which, though individually invisible to us, absorb in the aggregate a great deal of light, especially when the distance through which the ray has come is great, so that it has had to encounter a great number of them.

Now there is no means of preventing the loss of light from this latter source, namely, the absorption of it by substances floating in the air and thus diminishing the transparency of it. All that can be done is to increase the quantity of light sent forward, so that the distance may be greater that will be required to absorb it all. But the former—that is, the diminution by divergence—may be in a great measure controlled by means of lenses or reflectors so arranged as to collect the light from all sides, and send it forward over the sea in rays diverging but little laterally, and lying, horizontally, very nearly in the same plane. It is evident that they must not be in precisely the same plane, for the surface of the sea is not itself plane, but slightly convex, on account of the rotundity of the earth. The rays, of course, can not be made to *curve* in their course to accommodate themselves to this rotundity, and so it is necessary that they should diverge a little upward and downward in order that they may shine upon both near and distant vessels; and they must also diverge to a considerable extent from side to side, so that they may reach every ship, whatever may be the direction from which she approaches the land.

Reflectors are necessary for all that portion of the radiance which would naturally proceed toward the land, for it is only by reflection that light can be turned back directly from its course.

For a long time reflectors alone were used for the management of the light in these cases. They only served the purpose, of course, of intercepting and turning forward that portion of the radiation which was emitted on the side opposite to that on which it was required. The light which naturally went forward was left to pursue its own course without modification. It could only be modified by the use of lenses, and the difficulty of constructing lenses of a sufficient size for the purpose was for a long time insurmountable.

Contrivances for reflecting the light were, however, very numerous, and some of them were very ingenious and very complicated.

The engraving on the following page represents a system of reflectors devised to produce what is called a flashing light; for, in the case of beacon-lights that are not many miles apart, the luminous effects must be made to differ in some way, in order to prevent their being mistaken for each other. There are a great many ways of making these variations. The light may be colored by being caused to pass through red, green, or blue glass. It may be revolving or intermittent, or may be sent forth in flashes. In the engraving the several reflectors have each its own lamp, and they are arranged in sets of three (A, B, C) upon a vertical axis, which is made to revolve by approximate machinery, as indicated by the pulley on the

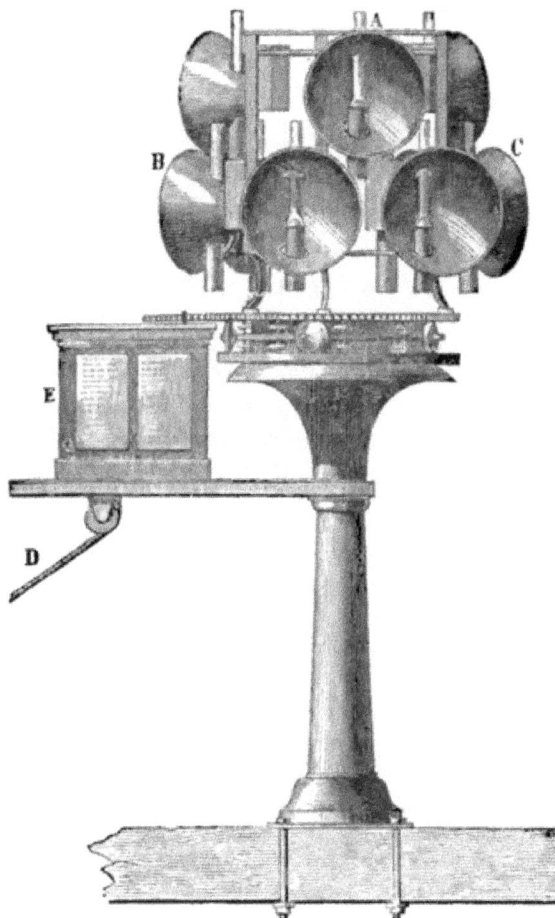

FLASHING LIGHT BY REFLECTORS.

left. The cord D, descending from the pulley, passes over another pulley not seen, and has a weight like a clock-weight attached to it. The clock-work by which the descent of the weight is regulated and the force communicated to the system of reflectors is inclosed in the box E. The little truck wheels on which the system revolves are seen beneath, on the platform formed upon the top of the stand, where they roll in a groove formed for the purpose.

The machinery is arranged so that the lamps revolve

very slowly, and all that is required to secure the steady continuance of motion is that the clock-work should be wound up every day when the lamps are trimmed, and set a-going when the lamps are lighted at night. Of course, as each set of three lamps comes to the front, their combined light sends a flash far over the sea.

A mode of constructing *lenses* of a size sufficient to be used in light-houses was at last devised by a French philosophical engineer named Fresnel; and so great was the success of his system, that it came soon to be almost universally introduced, and has connected his name indissolubly with the light-house system all over the world. Very great improvements have been made in his system by other inventors, but they do not displace his name as the originator of the idea out of which they have all proceeded.

It is only an idea of the general principle of Fresnel's invention that can be given in a chapter like this. It consists essentially in "building up," as it were, a lens for the concentration of the rays, by forming it in separate portions, each portion except the central one, and sometimes even that, being in the form of a *ring*, the surfaces of all the portions being so arranged as to produce the same effect in refracting the rays as if the lens was made in one solid mass.

To understand this clearly, we must consider that the function which it is required of the lens to perform is to *draw in* the rays somewhat from their natural divergence, since in issuing from the source they would, if left to themselves, diverge too widely. Now it is the property of a convex lens to produce this effect, as we see exemplified in the case of the sun-glass, so called, which is often used as a toy to concentrate the light and heat of the sun.

Now, to make a lens of this form, and of the size which would be necessary for a light-house, would require a very great thickness of glass in the central parts, all of which thickness would be useless in itself, since the light, in passing through, is changed in its direction only at the surfaces where it enters and where it emerges. It undergoes no change of direction while it is passing through the substance of the glass within. In other words, the w h o l e effect of bending, or, as it is scientifically termed, of refracting the rays, depends upon the angle *of inclination in respect to the surface of the glass at which the ray enters and leaves it.* Fresnel's idea was, therefore, to dispense, as far as possible, with the interior substance of the glass, by dividing the lens into portions, and making the several portions thin, while he still preserved in all the same *inclinations of the surfaces* in relation to the entering and departing ray.

CONVERGENCE OF RAYS.

You will see how this object is effected by the engraving, which shows pretty clearly the nature of Fresnel's contrivance, and the manner in which it operates to preserve all the refracting power of a convex lens by retaining the several portions of the surface in the right position in respect to the entering and departing ray, while yet the thickness of the glass is kept within reasonable limits.

FRESNEL'S IDEA.

The rays of light from the charcoal points to the left are brought into a parallel beam as they leave the lens on the right.

In this case, the rays, diverging first from a point, become parallel, which is the reverse of the case of the sun-glass, in which parallel rays—that is, rays sensibly parallel on account of the sun's great distance—are made to converge *to* a point. All refraction is in this way reciprocal. Rays subjected to refraction will always follow the same track in this sense, namely, that if they enter the glass—on the right side, for example—coming in a certain direction, and go out on the other side in a certain different direction, then, if the motion is reversed, and the rays of another beam come in on the left as the former went out, they will, on refraction, in the same lens, go out on the right precisely as the former came in.

It is plain that a lens modified on Fresnel's system, as above described, might be made of a circular form, as usual, in which case several sets of them would be required, forming different faces, to be presented toward different quarters of the horizon. Or the lens might be made annular, with a broad convex surface in the centre, and narrow ones in rings above and below. This last arrangement is shown in a simple form in the engraving on the following page, which represents a signal lantern such as is used on board ships.

These engravings are copies of those which Lawrence gave to John to put into his note-book, as illustrating in a simple form the fundamental principle of Fresnel's idea. John afterward found, when he came to visit light-houses on the coasts of France and England, that, in carrying the idea into practical effect, a great number and variety of most elaborate and complicated arrangements were made. When he went inside of some of the large lanterns and

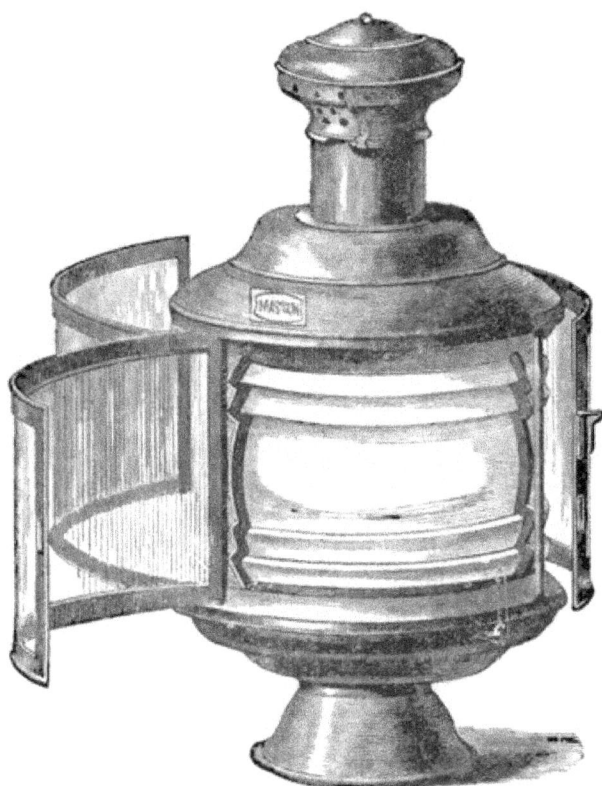

SIGNAL LANTERN.

looked around at the vast number of angular rings of glass
—that is, rings angular in section—and prisms, and groups
of lenses and reflectors, he was sometimes utterly bewil-
dered with the intricacy of the system, and almost dazzled
by the brilliancy of the effect produced by so much polished glass, even in the daytime, when the lamps were not
lighted.

He found that not only lenses, modified as above described, were used, but *prisms* of the same annular form,
placed above and below the limits of the lenses, were employed to bring down into parallelism rays which would
otherwise have passed out of range.   How this is done will

be shown by the engraving, where the rays forming the
centre portion of the diverging beam are brought to parallelism by the lens, and those that ascend and descend much
are partly refracted, but mainly reflected, by the prisms
placed in proper positions for this purpose, as shown in
section in the engraving.

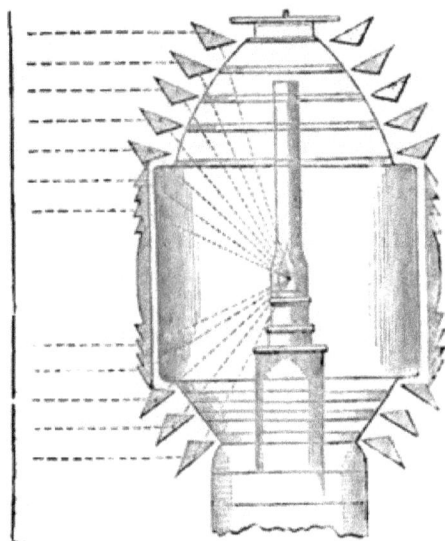

EFFECT OF THE PRISMS.

You will observe from the engraving that the light is
reflected from the *under side of the upper surface of the
prism*, where we should naturally think it would emerge.
It is very remarkable that it should be thus reflected back
through the interior of the glass again, instead of going
out into the air; but such is the fact. We can see a striking example of reflection of this kind by means of a tumbler of water. Fill a tumbler nearly full, then hold it up
carefully above your head, and look up at the *under surface*
of the water; you will find that you can not see through
it to what is above. If, while you hold the tumbler in one
hand, you hold the finger of the other hand above the top

of it, you can not see it by looking up through the upper
surface; but if you bring the finger down below the level
of the water, and on the farther side of it, then, with a little care in placing it right, you will see it reflected in the
upper surface *seen from below*—that is, from the under side
of the upper surface.

These explanations will give the reader a general idea
of the fundamental principles of Fresnel's invention for
managing the light in light-houses, and will enable any
one, when he visits a light-house constructed on these principles, to understand what he sees, when, without this preliminary knowledge, the complicated combination of rings
of glass, and mirrors, and prisms would form for him only
an intricate and bewildering maze.

Indeed, the number and the variety of the modes in
which these general principles are applied, and the vast
extension which the system has received since Fresnel first
introduced it, and which is necessary to produce the great
variety of luminous effects required for distinguishing the
different lights from each other, are such that it is the
work of a lifetime to understand the whole subject in all
its details.

Fresnel was a highly-educated man and a profound mathematician, and he made his discoveries, not by any lucky
accident, but by the most careful and thorough study of
the philosophy of optics. He was educated as an engineer
in the military schools of France, and was subsequently
appointed to important posts under the French government—first in respect to bridges and roads, and afterward
in relation to the establishment and management of light-
houses on the coasts. It was from the profound investigations that he made in connection with his official duties
that his discoveries and inventions resulted.

And yet, notwithstanding the great eminence as a mathematician and philosopher to which he attained, he was, when a boy at school, considered quite a dull scholar, on account of his apparent incapacity for learning and reciting lessons by rote, as was then, and still is, much practiced in schools. Yet he was, even at that early age, so much interested in the study of philosophical principles, that he had the name and reputation of a genius among his playmates, on account of his success in investigating the action and improving the forms of their toys and playthings, such as their tops, kites, and little cannon.

If I were writing a moral discourse in the form of a sermon instead of a scientific treatise, I might very properly close this chapter with two practical reflections.

First, that a boy, because he thinks himself smart in learning and reciting lessons at school, should not, on that account, become conceited and vain, and imagine that he is certainly going to become a great man when he grows up. Intellectual success and distinction in future life depends upon something very different from mere readiness in committing to memory, and fluency in repeating, mere words.

And, secondly, if any boy who is patient, faithful, and thoughtful in his endeavors to understand what he is taught, but finds that he is not so quick and ready in learning and reciting the lessons as others in his class, he has no occasion to be discouraged about himself. He may have within him all the essentials of eminent success in the acquisition of knowledge, which will develop themselves in due time.

I

CHAPTER XXII.

COLOR.

NOTHING can be in appearance more simple and uncompounded, or, as it is scientifically expressed, more apparently *homogeneous*, than pure white light. It was the celebrated Sir Isaac Newton who first called the attention of mankind strongly to the fact that a beam of such light can be separated into many component parts, strikingly different from each other in their powers and properties in relation to human vision. It has since been discovered that the radiation from the sun, which was formerly thought to consist of simple beams of light and heat, is infinitely more complicated than even Newton imagined, who only separated the beam of light into the seven principal colors.

The discovery of Newton was this: When light passes out of a rare medium like air into a dense one like glass, or water, or ice—or reversely, from any such substance into air, if it enters or emerges obliquely, the ray is bent a little out of the direct line, as you see very clearly when you hold a pole or stick in an oblique position, with the lower end of it in the water. The stick, seen from above, appears bent at the place where it enters the water, on account of the rays which come from that part of it which lies under the water being turned somewhat downward as they emerge, and thus are made to enter the eye as if they came from higher points within the water than they actually do come from.

For, as has already been explained, things always appear

POLE SEEMING TO BE BENT.

to us in the place from which the rays *seem* to come when they enter the eye.

This refracting effect upon rays passing in an oblique direction into or out of surfaces of water or glass has long been known. Indeed, it gives rise to phenomena which are to be observed all around us every day. Newton, however, in his investigations, ascertained that the light thus bent out of its course was, in some mysterious way, separated in the bending into *different component parts*.

The engraving on the following page represents this phenomenon in its simplest form. A beam of light from the sun enters through an orifice (*a*) made in the shutter into a darkened room; for, though this is not essential, the effect is far more decided when all other light except the beam to be experimented upon is excluded. The ray, in entering from the air into the prism (shown *in section* in the engraving) at *b*, is refracted upward, and slightly sep-

arated into differently-colored parts. In coming out of
the prism on the other side at c, it is
refracted more, and the component colored portions are still more widely separated. They go on diverging as they
recede, until, when they at length fall
upon the wall at d, or upon a screen
placed there to receive them, the rays

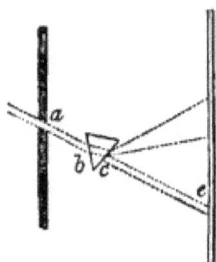

REFRACTION OF SOLAR RAY. which entered at a as a small beam of
white light form an elongated band of the most brilliant
and beautiful colors.

This band is called a *spectrum*. In this case it is the
spectrum of solar light, or the *solar spectrum*, that is produced. The spectrum of any other light may be produced
by similar means.

In case, however, the light to be employed radiates from
a point that is near, so that the rays are divergent instead
of being parallel like the sun's rays, there is an advantage
in passing them first through a convex lens to bring them
to parallelism before they enter the prism.

The number of colors which were developed in the solar
spectrum by Newton's experiments were seven, and were
called for a long time the seven primitive colors. It was
found that, by mingling these hues again by any suitable
means, the white light from which they originated was re-
produced. Thus the beam of white light, it was found,
could be separated by refraction into rays of seven different colors, and these, by being combined again, would re-
produce the original beam of white light.

There are many ways by which this reproduction can
be effected. One is by gathering the rays together again
from the spectrum by means of a lens, or of another prism,
in a reversed position. Another is by mixing paints of the
seven hues together upon a painter's pallet. A third mode

RECOMPOSITION OF LIGHT.

is by causing a disk with different sections of it, or, rather, different *sectors*, colored differently, to revolve rapidly, by means of a top, for example, so as to mingle and blend the colors in their impression upon the retina of the eye.

Of course, in both these last experiments, in order to secure complete success, it is necessary that the colors to be combined should be of the same hues and in the same proportions as those developed in the spectrum by the decomposition of the pure white light of the solar beam.

A top of suitable form, as affording a ready means of producing a rapid rotation, answers very well for making experiments in the blending of colors. Indeed, with a little ingenuity, a top may be contrived so that different disks may be fitted to it, and thus a variety of experiments may be made. The method which Newton adopted, however, was somewhat more systematic than this. He constructed a little machine to which his disks could be fitted, and thus made to revolve very rapidly by means of a multiplying wheel—that is, a large wheel turning a small one by a band.

The figure on the left, on the next page, represents the disk divided into sectors by lines drawn from the centre to the circumference, the several divisions being painted in the colors which it is desired to blend. When this disk is put upon the little axle made to carry it, in the machine, and set in rapid revolution, if the colors are of the right hue and properly proportioned, they all disappear, and the whole surface becomes apparently white, as shown in the central figure of the following engraving.

In process of time, as the solar spectrum was more closely examined, and as the instruments for producing it were made more perfect, and the arrangements for performing

NEWTON'S DISK.

the experiment were improved, the spectrum became more
and more enlarged, and the colors more separated, until at
length certain mysterious *dark lines* began to appear, passing across it in various places like black bars or bands
upon a colored ground.   These bands were found to be
fixed and permanent—that is, they were always the same,
and appeared in precisely the same positions in the spectrum, by whomsoever and wheresoever produced.   A celebrated optician of Germany, named Fräunhofer, first called
the general attention of the scientific world to this phenomenon, and after a time he published a colored map of
the spectrum with these lines represented upon it.   They
were thenceforth known in the scientific world as Fräun-

hofer's lines, and they excited great interest, though the cause and the significance of them remained for a long time an unfathomable mystery.

Fräunhofer gave names to the principal lines that he observed as soon as he found that they were constant and unchangeable in the solar spectrum, designating each by a letter of the alphabet. The names and positions of some of the principal ones—those that were first discovered—are given in the engraving.

The white band on the black ground represents the spectrum itself, and the lettered crossbars Fräunhofer's lines. It is only a very few of the principal ones that are thus named. Fräunhofer himself discovered and mapped many hundred of them, and the number has since been extended to several thousand.

It is now found that these lines depend upon the nature and the chemical composition of the incandescent substance from which the light proceeds. They are always the same for the light which comes from the sun, but different for the different kinds of artificial light; always the same, however, for the same kind of light. There are certain lines, it is found, that are characteristic of certain substances, and when these substances exist in any flame, or other incandescent source of light, the lines pertaining to them are sure to appear. Thus these lines in any spectrum constitute a language by which those who have learned it can determine with great certainty what substances exist in any flame the spectrum of which they have the opportunity to examine.

To examine the spectra of flames in this way requires a somewhat complicated and delicate, and very exactly made instrument. This instrument is called the spectroscope.

The form and general appearance of it is shown in the annexed engraving.

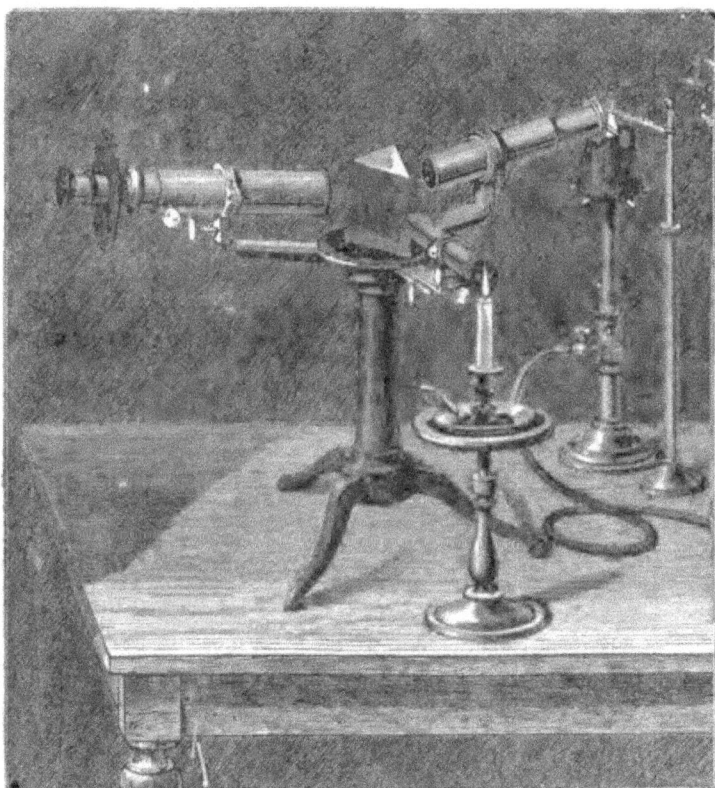

* THE SPECTROSCOPE.

It is only a very general idea of the character and construction of the instrument that it is necessary to communicate here. It consists substantially of a prism in the centre, supported upon a stand, and three branches in the form of telescopes directed toward it. The one on the right is for the light which is to be examined, which passes through the tube, and is prepared by the lenses contained in it for the prism in which the spectrum is formed. The spectrum is viewed by means of the telescope, which con-

stitutes the branch on the left. The third branch contains
a micrometer scale, so called, an image of which is projected upon the spectrum, and enables the observer to determine the precise position of any bands which may be
brought to view. By observations made with this instrument—spectral analysis, as it is called—the radiation which
comes from the sun, as well as that from many other luminous sources, is found to be of an exceedingly complex
character. The portion of it which constitutes light—that
is, which has the power of producing in our minds the sensation of vision, can be separated into a great number of
distinct parts, each of which produces a different sensation
in our minds in respect of color; and, besides the light,
there are rays of heat, and a third kind still, called chemical rays, a considerable portion of both of which can be
entirely separated from the rays of light in the spectrum.
Fifty years ago, a commonly received theory was that all
this radiation consists of streams of solid particles, which
were both inconceivably minute, and were projected from
their source with inconceivable velocity. The prevailing
theory at the present day is that they consist of different
modes of vibration or undulation, in an extremely rare and
tenuous ether, which is supposed to pervade all space, and
even to fill the interstices of solid bodies. The longer and
more slow of these vibrations—if the words long and slow
can be applied at all to movements so amazingly minute
and rapid as these are all supposed to be—constitute, it is
thought, the rays of heat. Those of somewhat greater velocity and minuteness form the light, while the most minute
and rapid of all are the rays of chemical action. In other
words, that the vibrations of the first class—that is, those
that are comparatively slow, have the power to affect us
with the sensation of heat; those of the second class have
the property of producing impressions upon our organs of

vision; while the third, in some mysterious way, act upon the principles of chemical affinity.

And here it is proper to say that, in reading works of science and philosophy, we must keep clearly in mind the distinction between the *facts* which are brought to light by the observations and experiments of scientific men, and the *theories* by which they attempt to explain them. Facts, once established by proper evidence, remain uncontroverted from age to age. We can rely with confidence upon them. But the theories are continually changing. They are only suppositions which may be imagined to account for the facts, and ought to be received with great caution. There is direct and positive proof that sound is produced by vibrations of some material substance, but there is no such *direct* proof in respect to luminous radiations. It is only a matter of inference and reasoning. The reasoning is, that we can only conceive of two modes by which a force can be transmitted through space, namely, by the *progressive motion of material particles*, and by an *undulatory movement of an intervening medium ;* and as it has been abundantly proved that it is not and can not be the former, we may safely infer that it must be the latter. It may be so; but then, on the other hand, it may be supposed possible that modes of the transmission of force can exist of which, having no experience of them, we can have, in our present state of knowledge, no conception. It is not very safe for minds as limited in their attainments and powers as ours to conclude that a phenomenon that we witness must necessarily be accomplished in one of two ways simply from the fact that we do not know of any third.

However this may be, the scientific world at the present day are almost universally convinced that the phenomena of light, heat, electricity, and the like, are all the results of a vibratory, or, as one of them expresses it, a kind of *shivering* motion of the particles of matter. But perhaps they are not more generally agreed in accepting this view now than they were in holding to the belief that these several principles were so many distinct material substances half a century ago.

But, whatever the truth may be in regard to the theory, there is no doubt of the fact that light is a form of force, which is transmitted from the sun or other luminous centre in combination or connection with *heat* and with *actinism*—as the chemical force is called—in apparently simple and homogeneous rays, which, however, in consequence of their different degrees of refrangibility, may be separated from each other, the ray of light itself being resolvable into seven or more component portions, which have respectively the power of producing in us sensations of the several colors. When any one of these rays enter the eye directly from the prism which has separated them, it produces at once and directly the appropriate sensation. If the spectrum falls upon a screen, or upon any surface serving as a screen, the several portions of it are reflected, and, entering the eye, they produce each its own proper sensations in this secondary manner.

The rays of light, besides being separable into their component portions in this way by refraction in passing from one transparent medium into another, are also subject to a somewhat similar modification—similar, at least, in some respects—when falling upon any opaque substances. Some such substances absorb the whole of the light, and reflect none of it to the eye; these are black substances. Others reflect the whole, though in a peculiar manner; these are white substances. Others absorb certain portions of the separated rays and reflect others of them, as the green rays, or the blue rays, for example—that is, the rays that are capable respectively of exciting the green or the blue sensation in our minds when they actually enter our eyes. That they are not green or blue themselves, but only have the power of exciting these sensations in us, is evident from the fact that, when we look out at a window through the air, although the blue rays, as we call them, are coming down through it all the time from the sky above, and the green ones coming up through it from the grass below, we see no blue or green unless we turn our eyes toward the sky or the ground. In other words, the rays have no blueness or greenness in themselves, but only have the power of producing the peculiar sensations to which we give those names when they enter our eyes and take effect upon the sensitive organization of the retina.

It is substantially the same with transparent substances of different colors. Green glass, for example, absorbs all those portions of the solar ray which have not the power of producing in us the sensation of green, while they allow those that have this power to pass. Accordingly, any thing that we see through such glass appears tinged with green.

Thus the color of any substance, transparent or opaque, depends upon the part of the solar ray which it reflects or transmits. And this is the philosophy of color, as at present understood.

CHAPTER XXIII.

FLIPPY.

I HAVE some doubt whether the readers of this book will be easily convinced of the truth of what I am going to show in this and the next chapter; but if they are not convinced of it at once now, I am sure that they will be in time, as they grow older and think more.

There is nothing that we are more inclined to trust in than the evidence of our senses, and, of all the others, there is none that inspires us with more confidence than that of sight; and yet there is no one of them all that is so fallacious, or that produces in us so many illusions.

When we are little children we see a reflection in the looking-glass. We think there is something behind the glass. We look, and find nothing there. It is an illusion. As we grow older we know that there is nothing behind the glass, but we are apt to imagine that there is an image or picture somehow or other *in* it. It is an illusion just like the other. There is no image or picture of any kind in the glass; the image is in our eyes, and nowhere else.

We look up at the sky at night—or, in fact, in the daytime when the sun is not too bright—and think we see a grand arch swelling above us. There is really no arch there; it is all an illusion.

We look at the dark cloud in the east, when a shower is past and the sun shines out upon the cloud from the west, and think we see a rainbow there. Illusion! there is no rainbow except in our eyes. There are causes in operation in the cloud that produce the image of a rainbow in our eyes, and that is all.

We look around us upon a spring or summer day, and
see, as we think, greenness in the grass, and other beautiful colors in the flowers. Illusion! the colors are sensations in our minds.

The sense of sight is perhaps the most fruitful source of
our illusions, but the other senses are in some cases equally
deceptive. We hold our hands before the fire and experience a sensation of warmth, and we imagine that there is
warmth in the fire; but a moment's reflection will show
us that warmth is a *sensation*, and that there can not possibly be a sensation of any kind in fire. It is sometimes
said that there is no *heat* in fire, and this is true if we mean
by heat the *sensation* of heat such as we ourselves experience by the action of fire. But the word heat has a double
meaning; sometimes it refers to the feeling which we experience, and sometimes to that *property or condition of
the external body that causes that feeling*. In the former
sense it is true that there is no heat in fire.

The word warmth is more exclusively confined to the
sensation, and therefore we can say in a more unqualified
manner that there is no warmth—meaning no sensation of
warmth—in fire. It is true, we sometimes speak of water
being warm, and it is perfectly right so to speak; only
when we do so it is important, in a scientific sense, to understand that what we mean is that the water is in such a
condition in respect to temperature as to create the sensation of warmth in us when we put our hands into it, not
that it feels any sensation of warmth in itself.

It is plain that there can be no sensation of any kind in
the fire or in the water, an idea which is quaintly expressed
in the well-known distich—

> "There's no warmth in the fire that heats you,
> Than there's ache in the stick that beats you."

In the same manner, it is true that there is no sound in

THE GARDENS OF THE TUILERIES.

the bell. There are *vibrations* in the bell which produce the sensation of sound *in us,* but no such sensation can exist in the bell.

Another very striking illusion may be created by the sense of feeling. If you cross your middle finger over the fore finger, and place a pea, or any other small round object, between the ends thus crossed, and roll it between them in the palm of your hand, you have a sensation of *two* peas, especially if you shut your eyes. The illusion is very strong if you perform the experiment upon another person—a little child, for example—not letting him know beforehand how many peas there are. Indeed, the effect is produced, though not so strikingly, by feeling of any small object, as the end of your little finger, with the two fingers crossed as above described.

No one will have any difficulty in admitting that these sensations are illusory, but I do not expect the reader will see quite so easily how our senses deceive us in the other cases of illusion that I have named, such as that of the colors in nature, the rainbow on the cloud, and the arch in the sky.

Lawrence was talking on this subject one day in Paris with John when they were on their way to breakfast, about twelve o'clock. In France the midday meal, which in the cities in America is known as luncheon, is called breakfast. They have dinner there at from five to seven in the afternoon. It is true that they generally take a cup of coffee and a roll early in the morning, when they first rise, but they call this simply "taking coffee." The regular breakfast comes about noon. Lawrence and John had taken coffee that morning at their lodging, and now were going to a restaurant for breakfast, and their way took them across the garden of the Tuileries, which are beautiful public gardens in front of the palace of the Tuileries,

and are frequented by great numbers of people every pleasant day.   There are broad and handsome walks, and groves
of trees, and seats, and smooth open spaces where children
play—the children being usually good-natured and very
polite to each other, as is the custom in France.

Lawrence and John were seated together upon chairs
near a massive group of statuary in these gardens, talking
together on the subject of optical illusions, and Lawrence
had already said to John what has been stated in this chapter, when John's eyes accidentally fell upon a group consisting of a gentleman and lady, with an elegantly dressed
boy accompanying them, who were walking at a little distance.   John did not recognize the boy as any person that
he had ever seen before; indeed, he did not pay particular
attention to him, as his mind was occupied with listening
to what Lawrence was saying, when all at once the boy
suddenly started and came running toward the seat where
Lawrence and John were sitting, waving his cap and calling out, *Sac a papier!   Vive la joie!*   He paid no attention to his father, who, in very earnest and authoritative
voice, was calling upon him to stop and come back.   John
did not recognize him at first, but he soon saw that it was
Flippy.   Those who have read the volume of this series
entitled HEAT will remember Flippy as one of John's fellow-passengers in crossing the Atlantic.

The shouts that Flippy uttered were French exclamations, common among French boys on such occasions, the
first being expressive of surprise, and the other of exultation; but how the phrase *Bag for paper!* has ever come
to be used for an expression of surprise would puzzle the
most learned philologists, one would think, to determine.
Flippy was beginning to learn French, and such expressions as these, when he heard them, made a great impression on his fancy, and he used them on every occasion.

Flippy's father and mother, as soon as they perceived that it was Lawrence and John, their old fellow-passengers, that their boy had discovered, came to the place, and seemed much pleased to meet them again. After conversing with them a few minutes, they took their leave, saying at the same time, "Come, Flippy."

But Flippy, who was not under very good government, remained on his seat, saying, "No, I am going to stay with John."

"But, Flippy," said his mother, remonstrating, "it is time for us to go to breakfast."

"Have you had breakfast, John?" said Flippy, turning to John.

"No," said John; "we are going now."

"Then I'm going with you," said Flippy. "Mother, you and father can go along; I am going with Mr. Lawrence and John."

Flippy's father smiled; he seemed to look upon a disagreement of this kind between Flippy and his mother as an amusing contest, in which there was no occasion for him to interfere.

"But, Flippy," said his mother, in an expostulating tone, "Mr. Lawrence does not want you; he and John have plans of their own."

"Yes, he does want me," said Flippy. "Don't you, Mr. Lawrence?"

"I don't like to have you disobey your mother," said Lawrence; "but, so far as John and I are concerned, we should like to have you go with us very much; and, if you have no serious objection, Mrs. Gray, we wish you would give him leave. Have you any?"

"Oh no!" said Mrs. Gray; "I have no objection; only you will find him very much in your way, he is such a heedless and troublesome boy. I don't think he really means to be disobedient; indeed, he usually obeys me ve; y well—when he has a little time to think."

So it was all arranged, and Mr. and Mrs. Gray, leaving Flippy with Lawrence and John, went away.

Pretty soon Lawrence and the two boys rose from their seats and began to walk slowly along on their way to the Palais Royal,* where they were to have their breakfast. As soon as they commenced their walk, John asked Law· rence to go on with what he had begun to say about illu-sions.

"He is showing me that there is no green in the grass," said John.

"He can't make me believe that," said Flippy; "I *know* there is green in the grass, for I can see it. Look there!" he added, pointing triumphantly to a beautiful green grass-plot which they were just passing.

Now Flippy was perfectly right in saying that he could see the green color of the grass. We all see it. But the question is, what is the *precise meaning*, in a philosophical sense, of *seeing* any thing. It means that a sensation is produced in our minds through the organ of the eye—a sensation, namely, of color—the *cause* of which is in the outward object, while there is, however, no sensation of color in the outward object itself, but only a mysterious something which causes the sensation in us.

"Do you think there is any prick, such as you feel, in the point of a pin?" asked Lawrence.

"It pricks *me*, at any rate," said Flippy.

"Yes," replied Lawrence; "or, as we say philosophically, it causes a pricking sensation in you, but there is no such sensation in the point of the pin; there is only that in it which produces the sensation in you. It is much the same with what we see. Greenness, as a sensation or perception,

* Pronounced *Pallay Rwoyail.*

is in *us.* The *cause* of it is in the grass, but there is no sensation of it there."

"I don't understand it very well," said Flippy, "but all I know is, that I'm sure the grass is green and the sky is blue."

"How is it about the image in a looking-glass?" asked Lawrence; "do you think there is any thing really there, when you think you see your face behind it?"

"Why—no!" said Flippy, reflecting a moment; "but that's a different thing; besides," said he, "there must be an image somewhere or other, and somehow or other there, for I see it."

Flippy's reply was not very consistent with itself, it must be admitted, as those whose convictions are controlled altogether by appearances, and by impressions made upon the senses and the imagination, and not rectified by reason, are very apt to be inconsistent. Truth is always consistent with itself, but error never.

After some farther conversation of this kind, the party reached the restaurant at the Palais Royal where they were to take their breakfast, and they were so much occupied with the scenes and incidents which attracted their attention there that they said no more and thought no more of the subject of illusions at that time. Flippy, however, was not at all to blame for being so entirely under the dominion of his senses in respect to his ideas of the real character of the phenomena that manifested themselves around him. He was very young, and, though his senses were in complete and perfect operation, his reason was yet only partially developed. It is only slowly, and by a gradual advance toward maturity, that the thinking and reasoning faculties become strong enough to assert their power, and to enable us to distinguish between what is apparent and what is real. A little child thinks the

rocks and trees are actually moving when for the first time
he passes rapidly in a steamer along the banks of a river.
He can hardly be persuaded that they do not move.   The
images of them do really move among each other *on the retina of his eye,* and he thinks that the objects themselves
must move.   If you whirl a burning stick in the air before
him, he sees a ring of fire, and he thinks there is a real ring
of fire there, if he is very young.   There *is* a real ring of
the color of fire on the retina of his eye, and he thinks there
must be a real ring conforming to it in the air.

When he grows a little older, he understands that in
these simple cases the appearances do not correspond with
the reality; but other illusions remain, and are only one
after another slowly discovered to be such, as his knowledge increases and his reasoning powers become gradually
unfolded.   I presume there are many readers of this book
whom it will be hard to convince of the illusory nature of
the deceptive appearances described in the next chapter.

CHAPTER XXIV.

ILLUSIONS EXPLAINED.

There are few persons whose ideas of the reality, in respect to external nature, are not still so far under subjection to the impressions of the senses that they are not easily to be convinced that the arched appearance of the sky is an illusion.

In conversing on the subject with John a few days after the breakfast with Flippy in the Palais Royal, Lawrence reasoned in this way:

"The arch in the sky, that looks so much like a reality, seems to come down to the ground at a distance of perhaps four or five miles from us."

John admitted this, only he had always thought it was farther than five miles to the place where the sky seemed to come down to the ground.

"It makes no difference," said Lawrence, "what we suppose the distance to be. Call it ten miles, if you please. Whatever the distance is, if we go to that place we shall find the sky as high there as it is here. Thus, wherever we are, we have a sky over our heads as high and as arched in one place as in another. If there were any thing real in this arched appearance, the whole surface of the globe would be covered with domes, like inverted cups, cutting each other in every conceivable way. This idea is evidently absurd. The truth is, that the dome-like form of the sky is an illusion. It results from certain laws in respect to the motion of light, and the effect which is produced upon our sense of vision by rays coming from dif

ferent distances and in different directions, so that the image of a dome is formed on the retina of our eyes when
there is nothing in external nature to conform to it."

Thus the vaulted appearance of the sky is the creation
of our senses, or, rather, of our minds under the illusive
evidence of our senses. The vault forms itself over our
heads wherever we are, and we carry it with us wherever
we go. Each person has his own sky, corresponding to
his own position, wherever it is, and it is a different one
from that of any person who is in any different position.
There may be many objects common to both, and those
which are at a great distance may be very nearly in the
same relative position, but they are really different; so
that, wherever we go, our senses form for us continually
an ever-changing sky over our heads, in which the objects
appearing in it that are comparatively near, such as the
clouds, kites flying, birds, and the outlines of distant
mountains, or the summits of spires tall enough to appear
in the sky, as we move, continually change their relative
positions, and some of them finally disappear, while other
objects come into view to take their places. In respect to
these various objects, there is for each a reality which produces the image of it in our minds; but as to the vaulted
appearance of the form which the assemblage of them assumes, it is all an illusion.

The nature of the illusion is partly explained by the fact
that objects appear smaller at a distance than when near.
Thus, of two ships, the mast of one which is near appears
much taller than the one which is at a distance—that is,
the top marks a much higher point in the sky, though the
one may be really no taller than the other.

We see this plainly illustrated by the masts of the two
whale ships in the engraving on the opposite page.

It results from this principle that, in the case of an ob-

MASTS OF NEAR AND DISTANT SHIPS.

ject approaching us from a distance, the top of it, while it
really remains always at the same level, appears to rise.
This is the explanation of the apparent rising of the clouds
in the western sky on a summer's day, and, in part, of their
increasing magnitude as they draw near. It is true that
clouds may, and often do, rise and descend in some degree
as ascending or descending currents in the air, when such
happen to exist, may chance to waft them. But any real
changes of elevation produced in this way are very small
and insignificant compared with the immense apparent
ascension of the clouds as they advance from the horizon
to our zenith. The whole of that, substantially, is a mere
illusion.

The nature of the effect is shown clearly when we see a
flock of birds approaching us in a long line. Those which
are near us look far higher, when we regard their apparent
positions as points projected against the sky, than those

K

which are remote. When the objects are birds (and we
know that, since they belong to the same flock, and are
consequently of the same species, they must be of substantially the same size), the difference of apparent size sug-

NEAR AND DISTANT BIRDS.

gests at once to our minds the difference of distance, and
so enables us unconsciously to correct the false impression
which would otherwise be produced; but inasmuch as, in
the case of clouds, of the real magnitudes of which we have
no means of judging, there is nothing to correct the sensible impression, their apparent rising, though an illusion,
has the full force of reality upon our minds.

The glittering colors which we think we see in the drops

of dew, which make us imagine that one is green, another
rose-colored or orange, and another blue, are also illusions.
Each drop separates the beam of light which strikes upon
it into its component hues, or, rather, into the different vibrations, or other forms of force by which the conception
of these different hues are awakened in our minds, and
sends them off in different directions, and the drop that we
see seems to be of the color of the particular hue which
comes from it to our eye. If we move our eye a little way
we come into a position when a different portion of the
spectrum falls upon it, and the drop which a moment before looked red now looks green. Of course, of different
persons looking at different drops, no two would see the
same colors in the same drops. A drop that would send
a blue ray to one would send a yellow ray to another, and
to a third perhaps no light at all.

Of course, when I speak of a ray of any specified color, I
mean a ray having the power to produce the sensation of
that particular color in our minds.

The case is somewhat analogous to this in the phenomenon of the rainbow. When there is a dark cloud consisting of falling drops of rain in the east, and the sun comes
out bright in the west, the rays, striking the drops, are
turned back by reflections and refractions, and are separated into their component parts precisely as they are by
similar drops of water in the dew. These different classes
of rays are sent off from every falling drop in every possible direction, so that the whole atmosphere—all around us,
and through the whole space between us and the cloud—
is filled with these innumerable radiations, crossing each
other in every conceivable manner, but without any sensible interference, or interruption of one by the other, or
the least confusion in the sensations of color which these
immensely varied vibrations, if they are really vibrations,

are capable of exciting in our minds. What takes place at such a time in the action of the sun's rays upon the drops of falling rain constitutes one of the most wonderful phenomena in nature—one the possibility of which would be utterly inconceivable by us if there were not the most irrefragable proof of the reality of it.

Now the manner in which these descending drops separate the sun's rays falling upon them, and send the different portions radiating in various directions in such a manner as to form upon the retina of the eye of any person looking at the cloud the image of a rainbow, is somewhat difficult to be explained. Sometimes a picture of a rainbow is made, with lines to represent the course of the rays drawn from it to the eye of an observer on the ground, who is also represented in the picture. But such a diagram tends rather to confuse the ideas of the student than to aid him, first, because it represents the bow on the cloud as a reality, when there is no such reality there, and, secondly, because the image of it in the eye could never appear to be in the same position for the observer shown in the landscape and for the person looking at the picture. The rainbow is sometimes even represented as foreshortened by perspective, as if it were a solid arch of many colors built into the sky. Now the idea of a rainbow *foreshortened*, as if seen obliquely, if not involving a contradiction in terms, is certainly a philosophical absurdity.

I shall therefore endeavor to give the reader some idea of the general principle on which the rainbow image is formed in the eye by means of the drops of falling rain, without any engraving to illustrate it, though I have several at hand made expressly for the purpose. I only ask the reader to imagine himself to be looking out at the door toward the east on a summer afternoon, just after a shower has passed over, and the cloud lies in the eastern sky, while

REFLECTION FROM THE INNER SURFACE.

the sun has just come into view, breaking through the clouds in the west.

In the shower-cloud in the east the rain is still falling; the sky in that quarter is full, in fact, of falling drops. As the rays of the sun enter these drops, they are at first refracted at the surface where they enter, and are partially separated into their component portions. When they reach the back side of the drop, some of them strike it at such an angle that they are reflected by the inner side of that surface, just as the light is reflected from the *under* side of the *upper* surface of water in a tumbler, as has already been explained. The reflected light, then passing out on the front part of the drop—that is, on the side toward the sun, the same by which it entered—is there refracted more, and the rays then come back toward the west again, those characteristic of the various colors being separated from each other, and diverging more and more widely as they pass through the air.

Now one would suppose that, this being the state of the case, the whole air would be filled with these radiating colors, or, rather, with the different radiations capable of producing these different colors, and that is the fact. But it is proved by the most exact and profound mathematical calculations that any individual drop must be in a certain precise and determinate position in reference to the observer in order to send the rays of any particular color—the green, for example—to his eye; and that all the drops which are in the same relative position will send the same rays to him; and those which are in the same relative position are those which come in the range of a circle of which the point opposite to his eye, in relation to the sun, is the centre—that is, the point determined by a line drawn from the sun, through the position of his eye, to the cloud. Thus, if a drop at a certain distance above that point sends a green ray—or, more strictly, a *green-producing* ray—to his eye, all the other drops in the range of a great circle drawn at the same distance from the central point above named will do the same.   But, as the sun is above the horizon, the central point of this circle, which is the point exactly opposite to the sun, must be below it, and, of course, less than half the circle will come upon the sky; but all the drops which come at the same distance from the centre in that portion of the circle which has rain-drops in it will send green rays to the eye.

Now it is evident that if an eye in any given position is in the range of the green rays from any drop in the cloud, it would be out of the range of its yellow or its blue rays, and that the drops which would send these rays to his eye would be for the one color above, and for the other below the one which sent him green-producing light.   Each of these, too, would have its circular band of drops formed of all those that were at the same distance from the central point with themselves, all of which would take effect in sending those component parts of the solar ray to the eye, which would produce there the sensations of their color.   Thus, while the whole sky is filled with falling drops, each of which is sending the same diversified radiations in precisely the same manner, only those radiations of any particular color would reach the eye of an observer in any one place which came from drops within the range of a circle drawn at a certain distance from the point opposite to his eye, and thus would be produced the appearance of concentric colored bands.

Of course, if he moves his position, he brings himself into a corresponding range of radiation from a new set of drops, and so changes the position of the rainbow in the cloud.   In other words, he forms the rainbow for himself, wherever he stands, out of the light coming from the drops which are in the right position in relation to the place of his eye. As he moves, he carries the apparent place of the rainbow with him, and two persons standing side by side see different bows in this sense, namely, that the rays that produce the image in their organs of vision respectively do not come from the same drops in the sky, and the bows are not seen in the same position. It would perhaps be too much to say that they do not see the same bow in any sense, as the question in what the identity of a rainbow really consists is one which might very naturally give rise to great difference of opinion.

It is, however, at any rate, perfectly sure that the rainbow is not an object real and fixed upon the cloud—one which we look at as we do at the cloud itself, or at the moon, or a star. As a real existence, having the form and appearance which it presents to our vision, it is an illusion. It exists only in the eye of the one who looks upon it.

Thus we see that many things which we are apt to conceive of external objects having a real existence, or as qualities of external objects, are, in reality, ideas or sensations in us. This truth applies to the impressions of the other senses, such as the hearing, the taste, and the smell, as well as to the sight. The words sweetness and saltness, for example, denote sensations, and, of course, there can be no sensation of any kind in sugar or salt. There can only be that in them which excites these sensations on the tongue which tastes them.

It is evidently so in regard to all the impressions made upon our senses. External objects communicate some form of force to our organs by which certain sensations are awakened in our minds, but these sensations do not and can not exist in the objects themselves.

Understood in this way, it is obviously true, as Lawrence said, that there is no image in the mirror, no bow in

K 2

the cloud, no arch in the sky, no green or gold in the dew, no color in the grass or the flowers, no sweetness in sugar, no fragrance in the rose, no sound in the bell, and no warmth in the fire, but only phenomena taking place in the external objects which have power to cause those sensations in a living being.

The conversation between Lawrence and John, which was interrupted by the dinner at the Palais Royal, was resumed after dinner. Flippy was quite interested in such portions of it as he could understand, and that evening at tea he put his knowledge to the very questionable use of playing a joke upon his mother. Just as they were ready to leave the table, he took some sugar out of the sugar-bowl with a spoon, and. wetting his finger, touched a little to his tongue.

"Why, mother," said he, "there's no taste in this sugar!"

"No taste!" repeated his mother, surprised.

"No, mother," said he; then he tasted it again.

"Let me see," said his mother; and, taking the spoon from his hand, she tasted it herself, very daintily, as if she expected that it would taste like salt. She found, however, that it was good, sweet sugar.

"Why, what do you mean, Flippy?" she said. "This sugar is all right; there is as much taste in it as in any sugar."

"No, mother," said Flippy, "the taste is not in the sugar, it is all in your tongue."

So saying, Flippy seized his cap and ran off, leaving his mother half vexed with his having played a joke upon her, and half pleased with his ingenuity and fun.

"Some of the nonsense he has got from Mr. Wollaston," she said, turning to Mr. Gray with a smile, "I'll engage."

CHAPTER XXV.

FORMATION OF IMAGES.

Light tends always to move in right lines in proceeding from its source. There are, however, two very striking and marked modes by which it is deflected or turned from its course. The first is called reflection, and the second refraction.

When the light, in its progress, falls upon a liquid or a solid surface that is *opaque*, a portion of it—sometimes a very large portion of it—rebounds, as it were. This is called reflection. When it falls upon any *transparent* liquid or solid, it passes in; but, except when it enters perpendicularly, it is bent somewhat out of its direct course in entering, and also again in emerging on the farther side, if it does emerge. Thus we may say, in general terms, that

Reflection is the turning back of a ray of light, or a portion of a ray, in falling upon a surface which does not allow it, or the whole of it, to pass through; while

Refraction is the bending of a ray of light, or a portion of it, in entering and leaving a substance which does allow it, or a part of it, to pass through.

Probably many of the readers of this book may have known this before, and they may also know some other things that I am about to state, especially those in respect to reflection. Indeed, some of these facts have already been referred to in a preceding chapter. But, even if you know certain facts individually and separately, it is a great advantage to have them brought together and stated in a systematic manner, so as to show them in their relations to each other, and thus, as it were, to connect what would otherwise be isolated facts into one systematic and harmonious whole.

To know facts separately, without any understanding of their connection with, and bearing upon each other, or of the general principles which they individually exemplify, and to act only upon knowledge lying in that form in the mind, is called *empiricism ;* but when the same facts are arranged in systematic order, so that their relations to each other, and the general principles which they severally exemplify, are brought to view, the knowledge becomes *scientific.* Accordingly, in what I am about to state in respect to reflection is intended to arrange in your minds in a somewhat *scientific* manner facts most of which, and perhaps all of which, you already know in an *empirical* manner.

When any opaque surface is plane, smooth, and highly polished, so that all the portions of it on which the light strikes present themselves to the rays at the same angle, each ray is reflected in the same manner—that is, according to the same law, and, after reflection, they all proceed in the same directions *in relation to each other* as before, though in relation to surrounding objects the direction of the whole beam is turned.

The consequence is, that light so reflected enters the eye precisely—in respect to the character and constitution of the beam—as if it had not been reflected, only it comes *from another direction ;* the object from which it comes of course appears of its proper form and size, and only seems to be in another place.

This is just what takes place when we see any thing reflected in a plane mirror. The engraving represents the course of the rays of light in such a case, taking those emanating from one point, namely, the tip of the flame, for an

THE PLANE MIRROR.

example. The light radiates from this point, of course, in all directions, though only the portion of it which ultimately reaches the eye of the observer is represented by lines in the drawing. This portion diverges as it leaves the point of the flame till it strikes the glass, which is seen edgewise in the centre of the picture, and then, after reflection, continues to diverge just as before, on account of the fact that the glass being *plane*, every ray is reflected in the same manner, and the whole pencil or beam continues its course, after reflection, without change, except in its *general direction;* and as the image in the eye of the observer is determined by the character of the rays *as they enter his eye*, the tip of the lamp flame will appear as if it was situated as far behind the glass as it is in reality before it.

It is, of course, the same with every other point, both in the flame itself, and in all the parts of the candle and the candlestick, although, to prevent confusion, those from only one point are represented in the engraving, and of those issuing from that point, only that small portion are drawn which ultimately reach the observer's eye.

The engraving thus fails to represent the facts as they

are in two respects: first, it shows an image behind the
glass, when in fact there is, in reality, no such image there;
what is meant to be shown is that the rays enter the eye
just as if there were such an image; and, secondly, the illumination from one radiant point only is shown, and of
those only that portion that finally enter the eye, while in
reality the rays proceed in *every direction*, both from that
point and from every other, those from each point crossing
those from every other point—every where—and in millions of intersections, which it would be impossible to represent in any drawing. Indeed, the case presents to our
conceptions phenomena so marvelous, that if we consider
every ray as a distinct and independent undulation, we can
hardly picture to our minds such a maze of crossings and
interminglings, made without disturbance or confusion, as
a possibility.

If, instead of a silvered glass, forming a proper mirror, a
plate of plain glass were to be used, the effect would be
substantially the same. It would, in fact, be exactly the
same if proper precautions were taken to prevent the transmission of light from the other side of the glass to mingle
with and confuse that which was reflected, or, rather, to
mingle and confuse the two sets of images which they
would respectively form on the retina of the eye. The several rays of light would not confuse or disturb each other
at all on their passage through the air. Each would pursue its own way unimpeded by the rest, and each set would
form its own image on the retina. It is only the mind that
would be confused in its efforts to separate and distinguish
the images.

If, now, the reflecting plate of glass, instead of being
plane and uniform throughout its whole surface, were to
be broken up, and the fragments thrown in confusion into
a basket, it is evident, as was briefly explained in the chap-

ters on spectres and ghosts, that the image seen in the fragmentary surfaces would be divided, and the portions variously dispersed; for the broken surfaces of the glass, being inclined to each other, would form different angles with the rays incident upon them, and would reflect them differently, and thus a mass of confused and disjointed gleamings would be the result.

If, instead of being broken into fragments of sensible size, the glass were to be ground into a fine powder, the particles would still reflect the light falling upon them, but the rays would be mingled in inextricable confusion, and, instead of producing any distinct images in the eye, or even distinct portions of images, they would only produce the impression of a general white light.

This is supposed to be the manner in which the sensation comes to us from any white substance. The composition of the surface is such that it takes up the light that falls upon it, and reflects it to our eyes in a confused medley of beams that can form no image on the retina, but only produce a general luminous effect.

If, however, we contrive by artificial means to smooth and polish any white surface, as that of marble, for instance, we can impart to it the power of faintly and indistinctly reflecting an image—that is, by the process of polishing, we form among the particles so many faces lying in the same plane, that by their combined effect they throw a sufficient number of rays, coming from any object near, in a regular manner to the eye, to form an image distinct, perhaps, in its general features, but faint, on account of these rays being mingled with others coming in confusion from the particles which are not in the same plane.

This, then, is the explanation of the manner in which the sensation of whiteness is formed in our organs of vision. A surface that appears white reflects the light that falls

upon it in a confused and irregular manner, so that it produces upon the retina of the eye no image regularly reflected, but only a general impression of light.

But some surfaces, which have such a constitution in respect to the disposition of their particles that they can only
reflect the light that falls upon them in a confused and irregular manner, seem to have in them some mysterious
power of making a selection among the rays thus falling,
and, while a portion are reflected, the others disappear.   It
is customary to say that they are *absorbed*—that is to say,
in the case of green leaves and grass, for instance, the ordinary white light from the sun falls upon them, but is not
reflected *as white light*.   Of the seven primary colors of
which the white light is composed, all but the green are
in some way apparently suppressed or extinguished.   The
green is reflected, and, coming to our eyes, produces there
the sensation of green.   So we say the grass is green.

It is, of course, an important and curious question what
becomes of the rays which disappear.   They are said to
be *absorbed*—that is, that they enter in some way into the
leaves or the grass, and remain there.   All light, whether
we can correctly picture it to our minds as a vibratory or
undulatory motion or not, is undoubtedly the action of
some form or some kind of force, and the prevailing idea
among scientific men is that that portion of this force
which represents green is turned back from the grass-
blade, or the leaf of the tree, into the air, while the remainder enters the tissues of the plant, and is there converted into some other of the numerous forms of hidden
force which is always in action among the molecules or
atoms of all substances, and on which the properties of the
substances and the changes which they undergo depend.

It is the same with all the other colored substances existing in nature or produced by art.   They have the power

of absorbing all of the light which falls upon them except that portion which forms the color which they present to the eye. And this, as was stated at the close of the last chapter, is the philosophy of color.

In respect to the regular and systematic reflection which is produced from smooth and polished surfaces, if the surfaces are *plane*, the rays are reflected, as has already been explained, in such a manner that their relative condition in respect to each other is not changed. The whole beam is turned out of its course, it is true, but without any change in its internal constitution, and the image which it is capable of producing in the eye is not changed in its form or in its magnitude, but only in its apparent place. When the reflecting surface is not plane, but is of some other regular mathematical form, as, for example, when it is concave, convex, cylindrical, or conical, the rays are reflected with regularity, so as to form images on the retina of the eye; but these images are enlarged, or diminished, or changed in various ways, according to the effect of the surface in modifying the directions of the rays in respect to each other. The eye, it must always be remembered, can take cognizance of the rays only when they enter it, and is wholly unconscious of any change of direction which they may have been subjected to on their passage.

There is a very curious piece of apparatus, called the magic telescope, which serves admirably to illustrate this principle.

There is a stand with a concealed channel passing through it, in which small square pieces of looking-glass are fixed at angles of 45°, one at each end. Above these ends are two upright tubes which have the appearance only of simple supports, though they are really hollow. Upon each of these supports are two short tubes, like telescope tubes, with an open space between them. In each

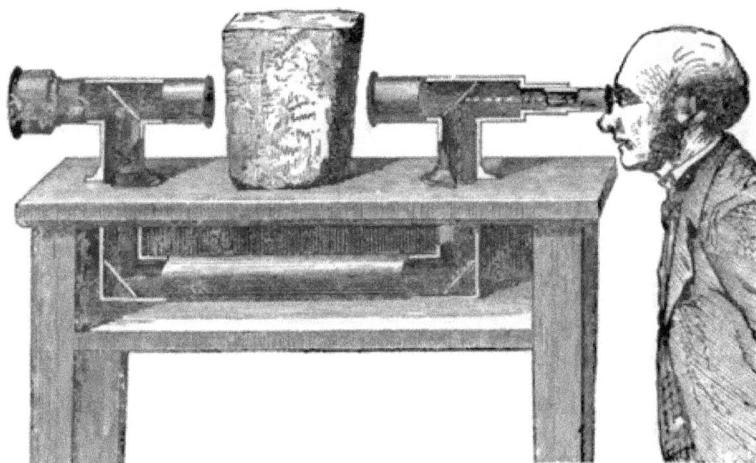

SEEING THROUGH A STONE.

of these tubes is a piece of looking-glass like those below,
and they are placed in such a manner, at an angle, that
light from any object—a candle, for instance, or a finger,
or a key—placed in front of one of the tubes, is reflected
down into the channel in the stand, thence along the channel, and up through the other tube to the eye of the observer. A big stone, then, or any other object perfectly
opaque, may be placed in the open space between the two
tubes, and a person looking through can see the candle or
the key apparently *through* the stone, by means of the
light which is carried down through the stand by the reflectors. The eye of the observer takes cognizance of the
rays as they enter the eye, and judges of the position of
the object from which they proceed solely from the direction in which they come in thus entering.

And so it is in all cases. By means of reflectors of various mathematical forms, the course and relative direction
of any rays can be changed in almost any conceivable manner, and made to enter the eye in any condition, as to direction and power, that the experimenter may please; and
whatever may be the surface which reflects any light, if it

IMAGE REVERSED.

is of a regular and mathematical form, the precise effect which it will produce upon the rays, and the condition in which they will enter the eye after reflection, can be calculated, and the kind of image which will be formed ascertained beforehand. Sometimes the image is diminished, sometimes it is magnified; sometimes it is multiplied, and sometimes it is reversed. The latter takes place when the rays are made to cross each other before they form the image on the retina, as may be illustrated by the image of a candle formed upon a screen in a dark room, after the rays cross each other in passing through a very small orifice.

The effects produced by the reflection of light in mirrors of various kinds, in respect to the conformation of the re-

ENLARGEMENT IN A CONCAVE MIRROR.

ecting surface, are very surprising and very beautiful.
They are all, however, the subjects of very exact, though
quite intricate mathematical calculations. If the mirror is
convex, it gives a diminished image of the object, as you
see when looking at your face in the back of the bowl of a
bright silver spoon. If *concave*, an enlarged image when
the object is held near, but a diminutive one if held at a
greater distance, as may be observed in the inside of the
bowl of the spoon.

If the mirror is cylindrical or conical, the image is very
curiously distorted; but the distortion is all subject to exact calculation, which is so certain in its character that the
reverse effect can be produced by calculating and drawing
a distorted picture such that when reflected it shall come
true.

DISTORTED PICTURE REFLECTED TRUE.

Toys are often made on this principle, as shown in the

engraving, where the drawing on the card below, which would seem to be a wholly unmeaning scrawl, is brought, by reflection in a cylindrical mirror, into a very significant image.

The study of the effects produced by the reflection of light from the various geometrical surfaces forms a branch of mathematical science of a very difficult and complicated character.

CHAPTER XXVI.

LAWS OF REFLECTION AND REFRACTION.

WHEN a ray of light passes from the air through any transparent medium which is denser than air, as glass or water, for instance, if it enters and leaves the denser medium at right angles to the surface, its course, it will be recollected, is not changed in its passage, but if it enters or leaves at any *oblique* angle, it is turned somewhat from a straight course both in entering and leaving.

Now we have seen in the case of reflection that, inasmuch as the direction in which a ray is reflected depends upon *the angle at which it strikes the reflected surface*, it follows that when the surface is *curved*, the different rays of any pencil or beam will be reflected differently, because the curvature of the surface makes the angle at which the ray is reflected different from what it would be if the surface was plane, and thus the condition of the rays in relation to each other is very materially altered by such reflection. Parallel rays may become convergent or divergent, and divergent rays may become convergent or parallel.

It is the same in respect to refraction. If the surface is plane, so that all the rays entering it are subject to refraction under the same conditions, they are all bent in the same manner; and if they at last enter the eye and form an image, the image is not changed in any thing except in apparent direction from which the rays forming it come to the eye.

This is what happens when we look at an object seen obliquely under water; it seems raised somewhat, but is not altered in shape. In the experiment of the bent pole, for example, the part which is beneath the water seems bent upward, but not otherwise altered—that is, the rays of light being all refracted in coming out of the water, without any change in their relative positions, but only in the direction in which the whole system enters the eye, the submerged pole is altered in position only, and not in shape.

Of course, as there is absolutely no limit to the forms of curved surfaces, nor to the changes in the character and condition of the different beams and pencils of light falling upon them, the phenomena resulting both from reflection and refraction are infinite in number and variety. To understand the subject fully, in all its possible ramifications, must, of course, transcend the power of the human mind; for the circle of phenomena widens and expands in every direction, and the facts run into an infinity of complicated details, where, of course, the finite powers of the human mind can not follow them. The study has, however, been carried very far by mathematical opticians; and the investigations which they have made, and the engravings which have been executed to illustrate the results, fill volumes. It would not be possible, in such a work as this, to give even a summary of these results.

There is, however, both in the case of reflection and refraction, a simple general principle on which all these results depend, and which it is important that every one should have in mind. This principle is in each case the key to all the phenomena, however complicated, and it enables us, if we possess it, to understand a great many wonderful effects taking place every day around us which would be otherwise mysterious and unintelligible. I shall explain these two principles as well as I can, first in common language, and then give the mathematical expression

L

of them, which we shall see is far more definite and precise.

In the case of reflection, then, the light rebounds, as it were, in a manner almost precisely analogous to the rebounding of a ball. If it comes to any surface in a sloping direction on one side, it goes off in a precisely equally sloping direction on the other side. If a boy standing before a wall throws his ball squarely against it, it comes back squarely toward him. If he throws it in an oblique direction upward, so that it strikes the wall above him, it rebounds upward, or tends so to rebound, in a line of direction pointing as much above as the line of direction of its approach was from below. It is true that the weight of the ball—that is, the influence of gravitation—immediately begins to turn it from its upward course, and soon brings it back to the ground. In the *actual rebounding*, however, as produced by the simple elasticity of the ball, the obliquity is equal on each side of the point on which the ball impinges.

It is the same with light. The ray moves off from the point in the mirror where it strikes in a direction just as far on one side as it came to it on the other. This principle has already been stated, and to some extent explained, in the chapter on "Spectres and Ghosts," where the operation of it was to be specially observed. The language, however, in which we have here stated it is very vague, and does not give the law with any degree of precision. The mathematical statement is much more fixed and determinate. The ray, in coming to the mirror, is called the *incident ray;* in leaving the mirror, after reflection, it becomes the *reflected ray.* The obliquity of its course in *coming* is called the *angle of incidence,* which is the angle made by the line of this course with a line perpendicular to the reflecting surface. The obliquity of its course in *departing* is called the *angle of reflection.* It is the angle formed by the line of this course and the same perpendicular.

The law, then, as stated mathematically, is,

That the angle of reflection is equal to the angle of incidence,

Which is only a more definite and precise way of saying that the ray moves off from the point in the mirror where it strikes in a direction just as far on one side as it comes to it on the other.

The diagram illustrates this very clearly. S S is the reflecting surface; I o the course of the incident ray, and R o the course of the same ray after reflection. The line o p being the perpendicular, I o p becomes the angle of incidence, and p o R the angle of reflection. The law is,

DIAGRAM. LAW OF REFLECTION.

that in all cases, and whatever may be the direction in which the ray I o comes, the line o R, into which it is turned by reflection, will always be such that p o R shall be equal to p o I.

If this law is once understood and made familiar, you will always see at once how rays will be reflected from any surface the form and character of which you know. If the ray comes to the surface in a line perpendicular to it, it will be reflected back in the same line. If it comes on either side of the perpendicular, it will be reflected back with the same degree of obliquity on the other side.

The action which takes place in accordance with this law, in the case of a concave mirror, with light falling upon it in one particular way, is shown very clearly in the engraving on the following page.

The point o being the centre of the curvature of the

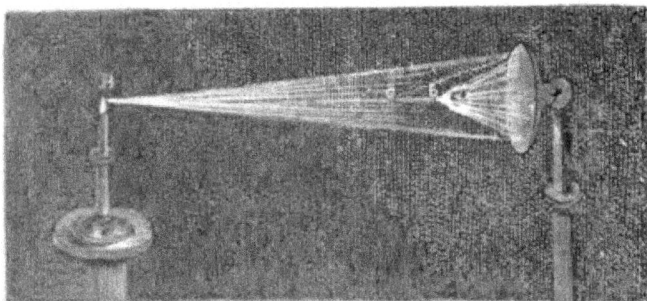

REFLECTION FROM A CONCAVE SURFACE.

mirror, every line drawn from it to the mirror will be perpendicular to the surface at the point where it meets the
surface. Of course, rays coming from any point to the
mirror outside those lines will be reflected *inside* them, as
is seen in the upper ray from the candle B, which, after reflection, must go to the point *b*, making the angle of reflection equal to the angle of incidence. If rays, instead of
coming from a near object like B, come from a more distant one, the angles of incidence would be greater; and if
they came from a distance so great as to make them sensibly parallel—as from the sun, for example—then the lines
of incidence would be farther from the perpendicular on
the outside, and those of reflection would be farther on the
inside, so that the rays would meet in a point nearer the
glass, as at F, which is called the focus of *parallel rays*.

This example shows clearly the general principle on
which all the calculations in respect to the effects produced by reflection are founded. Every thing depends
upon the position of the perpendicular in relation to the
incident ray, or, in other words, the angle at which the
incident ray comes to that part of the surface by which it
is to be reflected. Of course, as the directions of the coming rays and the forms of the surfaces may be infinitely
varied, the special effects resulting are infinitely varied
too; but this one simple principle governs them all.

In the case of refraction—that is, the modifying of the course of a ray of light in passing *through a transparent substance,* instead of being reflected from one that is opaque—the law is in itself equally simple, though it is, perhaps, not quite so easily stated. The best way for you to picture it to your minds is perhaps to consider that when a ray enters water, for example, obliquely, it has the *mass* of the water, or a larger portion of it, in closer proximity to it on one side than on the other *at the instant of entering ;* or, as it might perhaps be expressed, it comes sooner in contact, or *more fully* in contact with it on the side toward which it inclines than on the other side.

What I mean by this is shown in the diagram, where W *w* represents the water, S S the surface of it, and I *o* the incident ray. Now, whatever may be the nature of the force represented by the ray of light, and whatever may be the action of the water upon it as it passes into the water out of the air, it is easy for us to imagine that, in entering

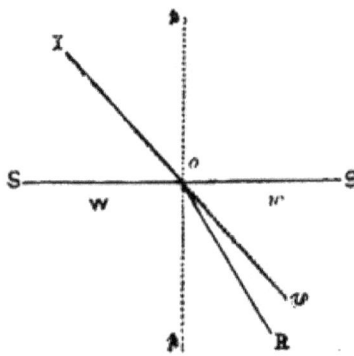

DIAGRAM. LAW OF REFRACTION.

at any point, as at *o*, it must come sooner, or more fully, under the action of the water which is on the side W, *toward* which it is inclined at the point of entering, than on the side *w, from* which it is inclined. Indeed, in former times, when light was believed to consist of solid particles impelled with great velocity through the air, it was thought that the bending of the ray to one side in this case was caused by the more powerful attractive force exerted by the greater mass of water on that side at the instant of entering. At any rate, this idea

makes it very easy in all cases to see in what direction the
ray always really bends in passing out of a rare medium
into a denser one.

In the converse case, namely, that of a ray passing from
a dense medium into a rare one, the effect is exactly the
converse—that is, a ray coming in the line R o, into which
the incident ray I o had been refracted, will, at the instant
of its issuing from the water, o, be *held back*, as it were, by
the superior influence over it of the greater mass of water
on the side W that is near enough to act upon it at the
moment of emerging, than by that on the side w, and so
will be *drawn down* into the direction o I, which is precisely the same as that of the incident ray. Thus the action
of the water on entering and departing rays is equal and
reciprocal.

This mode of stating the case is very indefinite and
vague, and would be wholly unsatisfactory considered in a
scientific point of view. It helps us very much, however,
in fixing in our minds the general law, to consider that, in
passing from a rare to a dense medium, the ray is bent to
ward the side where the mass of the dense medium lies
nearest to the course it is following.

Stated scientifically, however, the law is, that the ray, in
passing from a rare to a dense medium, is bent toward the
perpendicular drawn from the point at which it enters. In
passing from a dense to a rare one, it is bent *from* the perpendicular to precisely the same extent.

The diagram already referred to shows this very clearly.
The dotted line *p p* represents the perpendicular; I o is the
incident ray, entering the water at o. Instead of going on
in a straight course, as represented by the dotted line o v,
it is bent *toward* the perpendicular into the line o R. A
ray transmitted in the contrary direction—that is, from R
to o, instead of continuing, when it emerges from the water,

in the same direction, is bent *away* from the perpendicular and into the line *o* I.

In almost all cases of light passing from one transparent medium into another of a different internal constitution, the ray is bent on this principle. The effect in most cases seems to depend upon the difference of density in the two media, but not always. There is some mysterious quality or condition of structure, not well understood, on which the effect depends. The substance ordinarily employed for refracting light is glass, and a glass formed with curved surfaces to produce any of the various effects which may be required is called a lens. Lenses are of various kinds, according to the effect which it is desired to produce. A double convex lens, for example, is convex on both sides. Its effect upon parallel rays, according to the principle already explained, namely, that the light is bent toward the side where the largest portion of the substance of the glass comes nearest to it, or, in other words, toward the perpendicular at the point where it enters, is to draw the rays all inward, as we see is the case with a sun-glass, which is an example of a double convex lens. On the other hand, the same principle, in the case of a double *concave* lens, which is the kind used for the eye-glasses of near-sighted persons, will tend to *spread* the rays instead of drawing them together; for while, in the convex lens, the thickness of the glass increases toward the centre, in one that is concave the thickness increases from the centre to the circumference, and the light is drawn away toward the side where the greatest thickness lies at the point at which it enters.

It is easy, in the same manner, for one who has the principle of reflection in mind, as it has been explained in this chapter, to see in what way light will be reflected from a polished surface in any specified position or of any speci-

248   LAWS OF REFLECTION AND REFRACTION.

fied curvature. He has only to consider in what way *solid bodies*, impelled against such a surface, would rebound from it. Thus a concave mirror acts to gather together parallel rays falling upon it, just as a shower of peas falling upon the inner sides of a saucer or a bowl would rebound toward the.centre. On the other hand, a convex mirror will reflect rays in a divergent direction, just as peas falling in a shower upon the outside of a bowl, placed bottom upward, would rebound away from it in every direction.

CHAPTER XXVII.

THE EYE.

WHEN a child holds a buttercup, in a bright sunny day, under the chin of another child, if the light happens to come right, a slight yellow tinge appears upon the skin opposite to it.

There are two explanations of this phenomenon. One is the notional, and the other the scientific one.

The notional explanation, which is the one generally adopted by children, is, that the child on whom the experiment is performed " loves butter."

The scientific explanation is, that the petals of the buttercup having, in some mysterious way which no one pretends to understand, the power of separating the rays of white light which fall upon them from the sun into their component parts, and of absorbing all but the yellow rays, these yellow rays are reflected upward, and, falling upon the chin at a place somewhat sheltered from the bright light of the sun, are reflected to the eyes of the children looking on. This second reflection depends altogether upon the brightness of the light shining upon the buttercup and the relative position of the surfaces on which the light shines, and not at all on the taste or inclination of the subject of the experiment in respect to butter.

This case is a pretty fair illustration of the difference between the notional and the scientifical explanations of the phenomena taking place in nature all around us at all times.

The yellow rays, as we call them—though we must not

forget that what we mean by this term is, not that the
rays are yellow in themselves, but only that they have the
power of producing that sensation in us when they enter
our eyes—undergo, in the case of the buttercup and the
chin, two reflections: one from the petals of the flower, by
which they are separated from the other rays, and the other from the chin.   Any color may be thus reflected a second time, and the effect is more or less distinct according as the second surface is more or less shaded from all
extraneous light—that is, light coming to it from other
sources.   Thus almost any object held near a red curtain
which the sun shines upon will look red by reflected light.
In this case the red light from the curtain constitutes so
large a portion of all the light which the object receives
that the reflection of it becomes visible.

In the same manner, all the objects in an ordinary room
reflect each its own colored rays to every part of the room.
These rays mingle and blend with each other in passing
through the air, and if we hold up a sheet of paper as a
screen, they all fall upon it together, in combination with
the white light of the sun, so that the paper reflects only
a mingled and general light to our eyes.   But if a lens is
interposed in a proper manner between the paper and any
group of these objects, and all other light is excluded, then
the differently colored rays from all these objects, and from
the different parts of the same object, are made to converge,
and are brought to a focus, each in its proper place, and a
distinct image of the whole group is formed, with all the
parts in their proper position, and of their proper color.

How this is effected is shown very clearly in the image
of the lily in the engraving.   The rays from only two
points (A and B) are shown, but the same effect takes
place in respect to the light issuing from every other point
in the flower.   All these rays, in passing through the air,

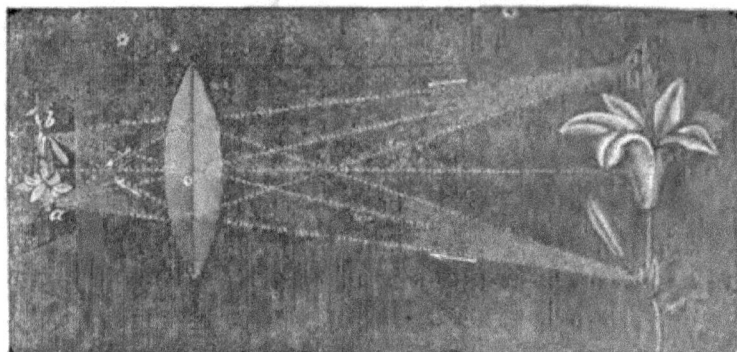

IMAGE OF THE LILY.

are completely intermingled, though each one, wonderful as it seems, pursues its way uninterrupted and undisturbed by the rest. A screen held at the place of the lens would receive them blended together, and would reflect their united light only as a general illumination. But the lens causes each separate pencil, coming from every different point, to converge each toward its own central line. The result is that the colors are all separated; and if the screen is held in the proper place to receive them, and all light from other sources is excluded, a perfect image of the lily is formed, only it is *inverted*, since the several pencils cross each other at *o* in traversing the lens; those from A, for example, coming to a focus at *a*, and those from B at *b*.

This experiment can be easily performed by means of any convex lens, such as a reading-glass, a sun-glass, or even one of the glasses of a pair of spectacles such as are used by elderly persons. Near-sighted glasses, being concave instead of convex, and so causing the rays to diverge instead of to converge, of course will not answer.

The only difficulty in making this experiment perfectly successful is that of keeping all other light except that which comes through the lens away from the screen, or from whatever serves as a screen, to receive the image

But if you make the experiment in the evening, and with only one lamp in the room, or, when there are more than one, if they are placed near together, and throw the image on the wall, or on a sheet of paper held near the wall, an inverted picture of the flame or flames, of beautiful distinctness, will be formed.

Images of any other objects, as well as of bright flames, can be produced in this way, if only all extraneous light can be excluded. This is exactly what is done in the eye. The eye is simply a space inclosed, with an opening in the front part of it, where a double lens is placed to receive the light, all other light, except the rays that come through the lens, being excluded. An image, then, of any outward object toward which the eye is directed, is formed upon a peculiar membrane at the back of it called the *retina*, which serves as a screen. Of course the image is invert-

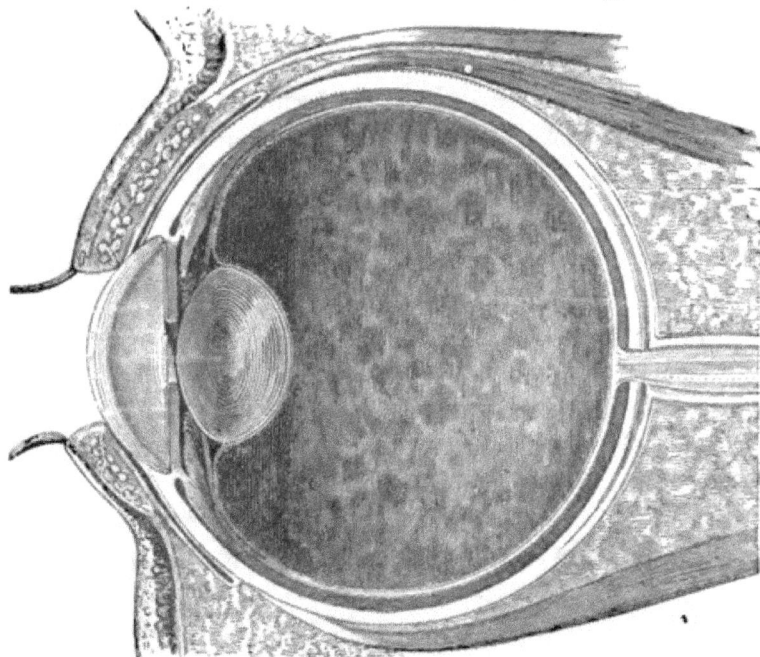

SECTION OF THE EYE.

ed. How it happens that we see things right side up when the picture that is formed in the eye by which we see them is upside down, is a mystery which greatly puzzles the philosophers.

If an exact model of the eye were made of porcelain and glass, with a little peep-hole upon one side, so that we could look in, we should see in the interior of it, on the back side, a most perfect and beautiful picture of any external scene or object toward which the opening in front might be turned. A great variety of optical instruments have been invented by man which act on the same principle as the eye. There is a lens to concentrate the rays, a screen to receive the image, and an inclosure to exclude all other light except what comes through the lens. There is also often a mirror to reflect the image, so that the screen that receives it may be placed where it may be most conveniently viewed.

There is another advantage in the use of the mirror in these cases, for, by reflection in it, the image may be thrown upon a *horizontal* screen, and in that case it may be looked at from the side that will bring it right side up.

There are many ways by which these arrangements are inclosed for the purpose of excluding the outside light; for, in order to produce the full effect, it is necessary that all light, except what comes from the objects to be viewed, should be excluded. Indeed, these instruments all take their name from the Latin words meaning dark chamber, or, rather, chamber dark, which words are *camera obscura*.

The following engraving shows one of the forms in which the camera obscura is often made. The rays R, which enter the tube B, are made to converge—that is, all which come from any one point in the object are made to converge, and they would fall upon the back of the box O, and form an image there, were it not that they are reflected by the

CAMERA OBSCURA IN A BOX.

sloping mirror M up to a sheet of thin paper laid upon a glass plate above, where the observer can, if he pleases, make a tracing with his pencil of the picture they produce.

Sometimes the inclosure to exclude light from the sides consists of a darkened room. The apparatus, however, for forming the image in such a case is substantially the same, consisting of a lens to form the image, and a mirror to project it where it is most convenient to place the screen. Sometimes the entering rays are reflected in the mirror first, and afterward passed through the lens. It is necessary in all these cases that the room should be darkened by means of shutters, or in some other way. The apparatus is usually fitted into an opening made in one of the shutters, while the others are entirely closed.

In order to avoid the inconvenience of darkening a large room in this way, a small building, like a summer-house, is sometimes devoted exclusively to the purpose of a camera obscura; this is often done in large public gardens or pleasure-grounds.

CAMERA OBSCURA IN ITS OWN BUILDING

Sometimes a camera obscura is fitted up upon wheels, like a traveling photographic apparatus, for a show; and sometimes in a tent, for the use of artists; only in this case it is necessary that the tent-cloth should be perfectly opaque and dark.

CAMERA OBSCURA IN A TENT.

The tent arrangement is attended with the great advantage that it can be removed from place to place, and can be set up in situations inaccessible to a wheeled carriage. In the engraving the tent is open in front, being drawn so in order to allow us to see the interior; and the cloth does not quite come to the ground, in order that we may see the supports. In actual use it ought to be closed entirely, except at the opening in the apparatus at the top to admit the light which is to form the picture.

The process of photography consists simply of *fixing* the image produced in the camera obscura. The box used is essentially the same with the one above described, but the paper on which the image is finally received, when all is ready and the picture is to be taken, is made *sensitive* by being covered with a chemical substance which is affected by the light.

There is an immense number of optical instruments, greatly varied in their construction and in the purposes which they serve, which, however, all depend upon the operation of the simple principles of reflection and refraction which have been explained. To enter into a description, or even an enumeration of them, would be foreign to the purpose of this work, which is simply to unfold and explain the grand fundamental principles that are exemplified in the action of light, as it exhibits itself to us in the phenomena of nature around us.

There is one principle which is, however, only in a secondary sense a property of light, which I must explain before closing this chapter, and that on account of the great interest which John and Flippy took in it, and in making a certain class of toys illustrative of it.

The principle is called the Persistence of Vision. The phrase denotes a certain property of the retina of the eye, or of the nervous connection between the retina and the mind, or rather, perhaps, a property of light in relation to these, by which the impression made upon the mind does not instantly cease when the image is made to vanish. Thus a succession of *very rapid* flashes always appear to us like a continued light, as the impression left by one does not fade before another comes to renew it.

A great many ingenious toys are constructed on this principle. The kind which principally struck Flippy's fancy—chiefly, I suppose, because he could manufacture them himself—consisted in making two different pictures on the two sides of a card, and then, by attaching strings at the

ends, and spinning the cards rapidly by means of the strings, the impressions of the two pictures would be combined in the eye, on account of the image produced by one not fading from the mind before the other came to join it. One of the pairs of pictures which the boys thus made consisted of a man on one side brandishing a stick, and on the other side a pig running away. Thus, when the card was twirled, you saw *one* picture consisting of a man driving a pig.

The boys made these pictures by cutting out the figures in black paper, and then pasting them upon the cards. The figures were not very well shaped, but Flippy said that that was no matter; they were just as funny for all that.

Sometimes they drew the pictures with pen and ink, and sometimes they painted them in colors. One which they drew consisted of an empty cage on one side, and a bird, which they painted of a bright blue, on the other. When the card was twirled the bird was seen in the cage.

The scientific name for this contrivance is the Thaumatrope.

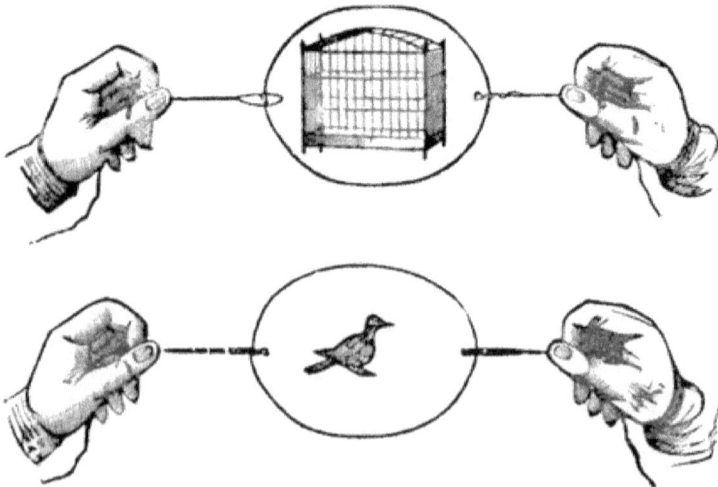

THE THAUMATROPE.

They also painted spots of different colors on the opposite sides of the cards, in order to see what compound color would be produced in blending them by the twirling of the card. The boys spent two whole days, during which they were confined within doors by rain, in making a number of these cards of various styles and patterns. They made them to carry home with them to America. Lawrence highly approved of this amusement. He said that such cards were worthy of being regarded with special respect, in view of their being capable of fulfilling a double function. They were equally adapted to interest children as amusing toys, and philosophers as articles of apparatus illustrating the persistence of vision.

CHAPTER XXVIII.

THE RETURN.

WHEN at length the time arrived for Lawrence and John to set out on their return to America, John had learned so much about the philosophy of light, both from the books which he had read upon the subject, and from the conversations which he had held with Lawrence, and he had, moreover, fixed so firmly in his mind what he had learned by the notes of conversations, and the other articles which he had written in his book, that he was greatly interested in the subject. Indeed, there were some indications, once or twice, as Lawrence observed, of his beginning to feel a little vanity and self-conceit in view of the progress which he had made.

After traveling slowly and by a somewhat circuitous route through France and England, Lawrence and John arrived at length at Liverpool, a day or two before the sailing of the steamer in which they had taken passage for America. The appointed day at length arrived, and they went on board with the other passengers, and the steamer set sail.

It was late in the fall when this return voyage was made, and the weather for several days was stormy, and the sea rough. On this account, and also because this was the return voyage, the passengers were more quiet, and kept by themselves more than on the voyage out—that is, *out* as the Americans call it, though the English always call the voyage to America the outward one, and that from America to England the voyage home. The Americans are usually much more quiet, and much less inclined to make acquaintance with each other on the voyage back to America, at the end of the tour, than when crossing the ocean on their way to Europe, at the beginning. They are tired of excitement and change, and their minds are occupied with recollections of the scenes they have visited, the pleasures they have enjoyed, the vexations and disappointments which they have suffered, and with thoughts of home.

After a time the wind and the waves subsided, and Lawrence and John began to come up oftener to the deck. One day when they were sitting there, about noon, waiting for the officers who were engaged at their observations to "make it 12 o'clock," and for the luncheon bell, which they knew would be rung as soon as the waiters should hear eight bells strike, John took out his watch, and, finding that it was after twelve by it, he asked Lawrence why they did not strike eight bells.

"It is after twelve," said he.

"But you have not got our true time," said Lawrence.

"Yes," replied John, "I set my watch by the ship's clock this morning."

"Ah! that was yesterday's time," said Lawrence. "We have run two or three hundred miles to the westward since yesterday, and it will not be twelve o'clock here until the sun has had time to come all that distance from where we were when it was noon yesterday."

John then asked some questions about the mode of making observations at sea. Lawrence said that the midday observation was for the latitude only, which they determined by the altitude of the sun at noon. The altitude of the sun, when it passes the meridian, varies from day to day for the same place, and it also varies with the distance of the place from the equator; so that by finding the altitude by means of the sextant, and looking in the tables, the particular latitude which gives *that altitude on that day* is readily found. There are, however, several corrections to be made.

Lawrence explained some of these corrections, and there was one—namely, that for *refraction*, as it is called—which John was much interested in, because his studies in respect to light enabled him to understand it very clearly.

It seems that the rays of light from the sun, in passing from the inter-planetary space into the earth's atmosphere, are refracted, and thus bent downward more and more in passing through the increasing density of it. This effect is greatest when the sun is near the horizon, and it makes the sun appear higher than it actually is. In fact, it brings his disk into view before he has really risen.

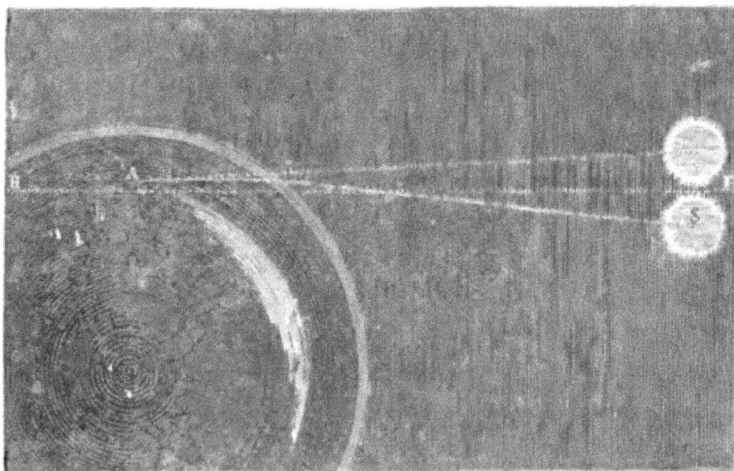

ATMOSPHERICAL REFRACTION.

This is made plain by the engraving, where the ray of light from the sun (S), while it is below the line of the horizon (H), is bent downward in passing through the successive portions of the atmosphere enveloping the earth, so as to come to the eye of the spectator at A as if it really proceeded from a higher point, and thus brings the sun into view while it is actually below the horizon.

M

The effect is greater when the sun is low, and continually diminishes with its increasing altitude; but the navigators' books contain a table in which they can find the proper correction to be made in every case.

John was quite pleased to find that he could understand this explanation, and the drawing which Lawrence made to represent it, so easily, and said, after a moment's pause, that he thought that he had learned a good deal about light since he had been on that tour.

"Yes," said Lawrence, "you have indeed. You have made an excellent beginning. But the field of knowledge widens more and more the farther we advance into it. You have learned a great many of the first principles, and these, being *fundamental*, are of great importance. But when you go farther, and study the construction and philosophy of the microscope, the telescope, the magic lantern, the stereoscope, and the analysis by the spectroscope of the chemical composition of incandescent substances, however remote from us, you will think that what you have yet learned is, after all, very little. And when you come to investigate the phenomena of *diffraction*, and *interference*, and *polarization*, you will almost conclude that you know now nothing at all."

"What are all those things, any how?" asked John.

"What they call *diffraction*," said Lawrence, "is a change produced in some mysterious way in the movement of rays of light when a very slender beam passes through a very narrow slit or opening, or by the side of a very narrow obstruction, so as to produce fringes of different colors. You can see these fringes sometimes, though very irregularly, when you look at a bright light with your eyes almost shut, so as to see it through your eyelashes. There are ways of producing them very regularly and beautifully on a screen by means of suitable apparatus, but to understand clearly how they are produced requires a great deal of mathematical knowledge. It is in some way by which the pulsations or vibrations of different rays mingle or combine their actions so as to produce new and strange effects. Sometimes two rays entirely neutralize each other, so that two lights make darkness. This is what they call *interference*.

"As to *polarization*," continued Lawrence, "that is more difficult still to understand. It forms quite a science by itself, and one, too, of a highly mathematical character. Polarized light is light which has been changed in a certain way, so that it acts differently from light in its ordinary state, and produces certain beautiful and very wonderful effects in the microscope, and reveals in a marvelous manner certain differences in the internal constitution of different transparent substances which could be discovered in no other way.

"What they call interference," continued Lawrence, "is, as I have already said, a kind of combination of the waves, by which the swell of one is made to correspond with the hollow of another, as it were, and so they are both extinguished. Imagine that you throw a stone into a pond and set in motion circles of waves, and then suppose that another stone is thrown in so as to strike at precisely the right instant to make a second set of waves that shall exactly coincide with the first set. This would tend to increase the height of them."

"Yes," said John, "I admit that."

"But now," continued Lawrence, "suppose the stone were thrown in at the right instant to make the hollows of the second set coincide with the swellings of the first. The two sets of impulses would then neutralize each other —or *interfere*, as they call it when speaking of light, and the water would remain level."

"It could not be done," said John.

"True," said Lawrence; "but can it not be imagined?"

"I don't think I can hardly imagine it," said John.

"Not even as an illustration?" said Lawrence.

"I don't know," said John, speaking doubtfully.

"You'll have to imagine it," said Lawrence, "if you wish to get an idea of what is meant by interference in the case of light. Besides, though you say it would be impossible, perhaps, to do this with waves of water, the effect can be produced exactly by a mechanical apparatus to make artificial representations of waves."

"I should like to see that apparatus," said John.

"At any rate," continued Lawrence, "it is found that rays of light, or luminous impulses following each other in a certain way, do extinguish each other. The experiments are very complicated and very curious, but they are thought to prove positively that light really consists of a rapid succession of some kind of undulations or waves."

"Do you think they do really prove that?" asked John.

"I think they prove the existence of some kind of intermittent action, with alternating conditions capable of intensifying or neutralizing each other, according as they agree or disagree; but whether the successive impulses are of the character of vibrations or undulations in a subtle ether, I do not know."

Lawrence was right, perhaps, in saying that he was not entirely satisfied in respect to the precise nature of this mysterious action; but, at any rate, it seems to be proved that there is an excessively rapid intermittent force of some kind or other that is concerned in the production of light, and the length of the several pulses, and the number which are produced in a second, seem to have been quite exactly ascertained, on the principle of determining the interval in time and distance which is requisite to produce

the nterference. The effects of this interference are manifested in many very remarkable and very curious phenomena. John said that he should like to see some of them.
Lawrence replied that it was easy to see them, but not so
easy to understand how they were produced.

"They appear in various colored fringes," said Lawrence, "in almost all transparent substances which are
made extremely thin—so thin that the light, in being reflected back and forth from one surface to the other, is
caused to 'interfere.' We can make a thin film of air
which will show them by pressing two plates of glass together which have surfaces that are not exactly parallel.
We see them in very thin plates of mica, and in a thin film
of oil or other such substance, floating upon water; and,

BLOWING BUBBLES.

better still, children observe and admire them in the soap bubbles which they blow. The colors come out when the bubble grows so large that the water inclosing it becomes extremely thin.

"I have seen the colors in the bubbles very often," said John, "but I don't understand how they can be produced by any kind of interference of waves."

"No," replied Lawrence, "I do not wonder that you do not. It requires a very profound mathematical study to understand it. Newton studied it in that way—"

"What! with a soap-bubble?" asked John.

"Yes," replied Lawrence; "but the colors moved about so much when the bubble was floating in the open air, and the water dried from the surface so as to cause it to burst so soon, that at first he met with a good deal of difficulty. He saw that it was necessary to contrive some way to remedy these evils, so he blew his bubble in a glass globe, with very transparent sides, which served to protect it from the air, and which he previously filled with moist air in order to prevent the evaporation."

He found that, when thus covered, the bubble was much more permanent than when exposed in the open air, and the colors arranged themselves in the most symmetrical and beautiful manner.

"I mean to try it when I get home," said John.

"I would do so, if I were you," replied Lawrence.

"Only," said John, "I don't know how I can get a glass globe."

"Any kind of bottle or jar would do, I suppose," said Lawrence; "only you must have a stopper, and pass the tube that you blow your bubble with through it, so as to keep the moisture all in the jar, in order to prevent the water of the bubble from evaporating. You must also stop the opening into the pipe, for there is a certain con-

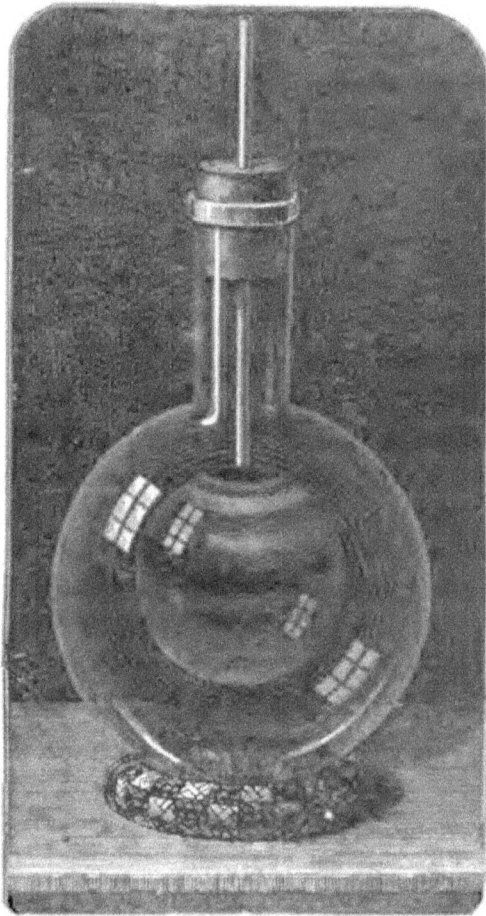

NEWTON'S BUBBLE.

tractile force in a bubble which gradually begins to drive
the air out of it when you stop blowing in, if you leave the
pipe open.   You see this by the bubble's growing gradually smaller and smaller."

When Lawrence and John had arrived at about this
point in their conversation, the officer in charge struck
eight bells.   Those who had been making observations immediately went below with their sextants and the lunch-
eon-bell rang.

The voyage went on very smoothly and pleasantly after this, though every one seemed more than usually impatient to reach the land.

At length, just before the time arrived for the land to come in sight, a pilot-boat appeared. The passengers were all very much interested in the coming of the pilot, for they expected that he would bring them the news which had been passing under the Atlantic from Europe to America, on the telegraph wire, since they left Liverpool; and as this was the year of the great French and German war, they were very anxious to learn what had happened since they left the English shores. When the pilot came, however, they were much disappointed at learning that his boat left New York only the day after the steamer had left Liverpool, so that he could give the passengers only one day's later news.

It was a joyful hour for all the passengers when the steamer was sailing up the harbor. Home seemed to them more attractive, after all, than any of the scenes of novelty and beauty which had enticed them abroad.

The immense steamer came up very slowly and with much difficulty to the pier. There were many lines taken out in boats to the pier and fastened there, and hard pulling upon them by the sailors at windlasses and capstans, and much alternate stopping, and backing, and going forward of the engine. There were crowds of people all this time upon the pier waving hats and handkerchiefs, which salutations were responded to by the passengers on board, who crowded the promenade deck and leaned over the railings at every point where they could see.

At length the bow of the steamer was brought up in an awkward position among the piles at the head of the pier, and a broad plank platform was laid across for the transfer of the baggage on shore. There were no facilities yet for

the passengers to land, or for any of their friends to come
on board. A few adventurous gentlemen, however, more
bold or more agile than the rest, were soon seen clamber-
ing up over the piles and getting from them into the rigging, so as to come on board. Among them John's eye
fell upon a boy who was stopping one of these gentlemen
and asking him to give him his hand to help him across a
very dangerous place.

"Look! Lawrence, look!" said John; "there's Flippy!
I verily believe that's Flippy!"

It was indeed Flippy. He had seen in the newspaper
the names of Lawrence and John in the list of the passengers that were to cross the Atlantic in that steamer, which
had been telegraphed to New York, and, being in New
York at the time, had come down to welcome them to
their native land.

M 2

CHAPTER XXIX.

FAREWELL TO FLIPPY.

A FEW days after the return of Lawrence and John to New York, they went on board a North River steam-boat to go up the river on their way to their home in the country.

It was late in the afternoon when they went on board. On their way from the hotel to the pier, John said to Lawrence, in the carriage,

"It would have been better for us to have planned to go up in the day-boat."

"Why so?" asked Lawrence.

"Because then we could have seen the scenery better," said John.

"That is not a settled question," replied Lawrence. "Some people think that the scenery in the evening, by starlight or moonlight, is a great deal more grand and sublime, especially in passing through the Highlands."

"I don't care much about that," said John. "I like to see them stop at the landings, and watch the people going off and the others coming on in the day-time, when I can see them plainly."

"Yes," rejoined Lawrence, "I should expect that you would take more interest in such scenes now than in mountains by moonlight. You have not yet attained to the romantic age."

"The romantic age?" repeated John.

"Yes," said Lawrence. "I divide the period of childhood and youth into four ages. First comes the Wondering Age, then the Noisy Age, then the Teasing Age, and, last of all, the Romantic Age. The Romantic Age has not come for you yet."

At this point in the conversation the carriage stopped. They had arrived, it seemed, at the pier. So they descended from the carriage, and, after paying the fare and attending to their baggage, they went on board.

"Lead the way, John," said Lawrence, as they stepped from the gang-plank to the deck, "and find the place where you would like to sit. We have more than half an hour yet before the steamer will start."

John replied that he would like to sit where he could see the people come on board; and, so saying, he led the way up to the after promenade deck, and there, choosing two comfortable arm-chairs, he brought them to the side of the deck next the pier, where he could see the carriages and carts as they arrived, and the foot people, and the orange-women, and the news-boys, and witness at his ease all the exciting scenes and incidents which usually attend the sailing of a North River steamer from a New York pier. As soon as he and Lawrence were comfortably established in their seats, he asked Lawrence to go on with what he was saying about the ages of childhood and youth.

So Lawrence went on to explain what he meant by the various ages that he had specified. The Wondering Age, he said, continued from infancy till the boy was seven or eight years old. Up to that time the world was all new to him, and his mind was chiefly occupied with curiosity and wonder. He went about prying into every thing. He believed every thing that he heard, so that it was very easy to make a fool of him. He liked fairy tales, and the more absurd and impossible they were, the better he was pleased with them.

"Next comes the period from seven or eight to ten or

twelve," continued Lawrence, "which I call the Noisy Age. The boy has by this time become somewhat accustomed to the strange world that he finds himself brought into, and feels more at home in it, and begins to see more clearly the difference between truth and falsehood in it. His powers and faculties have become enlarged and developed, his strength is increased, and he begins to like to produce sensations and effects. One of the easiest effects that he can produce is noise. He likes to hear it, and he makes a great deal of it. Indeed, the more bustle and noise there is, the better, especially if he makes it himself. So I call this the Noisy Age. In this age the boy, if left to himself, and is strong and healthy, breaks into a room rudely where people are quietly talking, and if reproved and asked to be more quiet, he goes out sometimes slamming the door, and making more noise in going out than he did in coming in."

"Yes," said John, smiling, and at the same time looking a little ashamed, "I used to do so."

"In this age, too," continued Lawrence, "boys are fond of rough and noisy plays. They are always pushing each other, chasing each other, and tripping each other up, with a vast amount of shouting and hallooing by way of musical accompaniment.

"Next comes the Teasing Age," continued Lawrence. "The boy's mental faculties have now become somewhat more fully developed, and the effects that he now likes to produce are such as relate somewhat more to the minds of people than merely to their eyes and ears. He takes special pleasure in making fools of people, in getting boys or dumb animals angry with each other, and seeing them fight. If he has any sisters, he seems sometimes to take special pleasure in teasing them. That is the reason why I call it the Teasing Age."

ROUGH PLAYS.

"I think you ought to call it the Ugly Age," said John.

"No," rejoined Lawrence, "it is not exactly from a spirit of ugliness that he does these things, but only from the pleasure of exercising his growing powers in new forms. To produce a disturbance or an excitement in a person's mind involves the exercise of a higher class of faculties than merely to make a din in their ears, and the boy likes to exercise his highest powers. The Teásing Age comes generally between ten or twelve and sixteen. After sixteen the boy generally becomes too much of a gentleman to take pleasure in troubling people in any way, especially his sisters. He then becomes ambitious of making himself agreeable instead of disagreeable."

"*I'm* between ten and sixteen," said John, "so I am in the Teasing Age."

"Your case is an exception to the general rule," said Lawrence.

"I think there are a great many exceptions," said John.

"I think so too," replied Lawrence; "indeed, it would not be a good specimen of a general rule if there were not a great many exceptions."

"Look! look! Lawrence," said John, suddenly interrupting and pointing toward the pier; "there comes Flippy!"

It was indeed Flippy. He was coming down the pier with a parcel in his hand. John ran to meet him.

In a few minutes he returned, bringing Flippy to the place where Lawrence was sitting. Flippy placed his parcel in Lawrence's hands, saying at the same time,

"There is something for you; but you must not open it until you get home."

"Is it a present for me from you?" asked Lawrence.

"Yes," replied Flippy; "though my father gave me the money to buy it, because you were so kind to me and taught me so much while we were on the voyage. And I want to go home with you now," he continued, "to where you live."

"Oh no!" rejoined Lawrence; "it is too far; it is more than two hundred miles from here."

"No matter for that," said Flippy; "I can write back to my father at the first place where we stop, and he will send me some money. He won't care, so long as he knows that I am with you."

"But your mother would care," replied Lawrence; "she would be very anxious and very much worried about you."

"No matter," said Flippy. "She would find out after a while that I was all right."

Lawrence replied that, though his mother might find out that he was all right, as he called it, in the end, she would endure a great deal of suffering in the mean time through her suspense and anxiety; and then, in order to see if he could not awaken some sentiment of gratitude in his mind toward his mother, he reminded him of his obligations to her for all the care and trouble which she had borne for him in former years, when he was a little child; how she had attended him and watched over him in sickness, and sat by his bedside at night, and provided for all his wants.

"My mother never did any of those things for me," said Flippy.

"Who did them, then?" asked Lawrence.

"Bonney," replied the boy.

"And who was Bonney?" asked Lawrence.

"She was a girl, or perhaps a woman," said Flippy. "My mother called her the *bonne*, but I generally called her Bonney—generally, but not always, for sometimes when she scolded me I used to call her Bony."

"Did she use to scold you?" asked Lawrence.

"Sometimes," said Flippy, "especially when she caught me sliding down the banisters."

FLIPPY WHEN HE WAS LITTLE.

"It seems to me it was hardly right to call her a bad

name," said Lawrence, "because she wished to prevent you from sliding down the banisters. It was only out of regard for your safety that she did it. I knew a boy once who fell and broke his leg by sliding down the banisters."

"I know," said Flippy; "but I could poise myself exactly; besides, it was not a very bad name for her, for she was really rather bony."

Just at this moment the bell rang, and a steward called out, "All ashore that's going!" So Flippy rose, and, bidding Lawrence good-by, he and John went down the companion-way to the main deck, and there Flippy fell into the current of people that were pouring in a continued stream over the plank to the pier. The last thing that Flippy said was that he wished Lawrence had allowed him to go with him and John.

"I might have gone just as well as not," said he, "and I could have written to my father at the first stopping-place to send me some money and a trunk full of clothes."

Before John had made his way back to where Lawrence was sitting, the steam-boat had begun to move away from the pier, and very soon began to glide very swiftly past the long line of ships, and ferry-boats, and canal-boats, and sloops which lay at the wharves and filled the docks which here formed the margin of the river.

"I like Flippy pretty well," said John, as soon as he had resumed his seat, "but I don't think he is very grateful to his mother."

"It is partly because he does not know how much she has done and suffered for him," replied Lawrence. "There seems to be a principle of gratitude in his heart, or else he would not have thought of bringing a present to me, on account, as he says, of my having been kind to him."

Here Lawrence held up the parcel which Flippy had given him, and which was still lying in his lap.

"What I have done for him," he added, "little as it is, he knows and appreciates, and so he is grateful for it. But his mother has perhaps not done much to win his affections of late years. It is very likely that, since he was old enough to be put under the charge of a *bonne*, she has not had much to do with him except to watch him and check him when he is doing any thing wrong, and he has not the least idea how much she must have done and suffered for him before that time. What he wants is *light*. When he grows older, and understands how much he owes his mother, it is very probable that he will be grateful for it all, and he may then become a great comfort to her. I am sure I hope he will."

"I wonder what the present is that he has brought for you!" said John. "Let's open it now."

"No," replied Lawrence; "I was not to open it till we got home."

Here John took up the parcel and began to feel of it, in hopes of being able to ascertain in that way what it was.

"I thought it was books," said he, "but it is some kind of box—a pasteboard box. I wonder what is in it! If I were you, I would open it now and see."

"I was not to open it until we got home," said Lawrence.

"You did not promise him that you would not," replied John.

"No," rejoined Lawrence, "I did not promise in words, but I received the package on that implied condition."

"He would not care," said John. "All he wanted was that you should not open it while he was by. I don't see what possible harm it could do for you to open it now."

"I do," said Lawrence.

"What harm?" asked John.

"Guess," said Lawrence.

"That it might be some delicate thing that would get injured by being opened here?" suggested John, speaking in the tone of a question.

"That is a pretty good reason," said Lawrence, "but that is not what I meant."

"Then I give it up," rejoined John.

"It would injure my credit and character for trustworthiness and faithfulness with you," said Lawrence. "If you found that I would take a thing from Flippy on certain conditions, understood, and then would not observe the conditions because he was not there to see, you could never have full confidence in my faithfully fulfilling any conditions that I should make with *you.*"

John pondered somewhat thoughtfully upon this view of the case, but he did not reply. Indeed, it was pretty evident that there was nothing that could be very well said in reply.

Lawrence attached great importance to the idea of sustaining the character of perfect trustworthiness in the estimation of all who knew him. He was particularly desirous that John should at all times have entire confidence in him. He knew, moreover, that the only sure way of making all who know us *believe* that we are thoroughly honest and true, is to *be* in reality thoroughly honest and true.

CHAPTER XXX.

UP THE NORTH RIVER.

For twenty or thirty miles above New York, the North River, as it is there called, is of its ordinary width, and runs in a pretty straight course, with a range of lofty and precipitous cliffs on one side, and a series of charming landscapes, consisting of groves, gardens, pleasure-grounds, villas, public institutions, and pretty little landings leading to them, on the other. For an hour after leaving the pier at New York, Lawrence and John remained at their seats upon the upper deck, in the midst of many animated groups formed of the other passengers—some talking, some reading, some sitting quietly in silence, but all enjoying the mild and balmy air of the evening and the beauty of the scenery.

"Why do they call this river the North River in New York," asked John, "while every where else it is called the Hudson River?"

"That is certainly very singular," said Lawrence.

"Even the same people," continued John, "call it the North River when they are here, and call it the Hudson River when they are in Boston."

"Not always," said Lawrence.

"No, not always," replied John; "but why do they ever? What is the use of having two names for the same river at all?"

"It is very common," said Lawrence, "to have two names for the same thing, to be used indiscriminately; but this seems to be a case where the use of one word or the other depends in some degree upon the place we happen to be in when we use it. That's a curious philological phenomenon."

"Philological?" repeated John.

"Yes," replied Lawrence; "philology is the science that treats of the origin and the meaning of words, and the changes they undergo in the spelling and the use of them. It is a very curious subject. You will be very much interested in studying it one of these days, when you get older."

"Should not I be interested in it now?" asked John.

"Perhaps so," replied Lawrence. "You might try. You might begin by looking into the histories of New York and of the early settlements of this country, and see if you can find out when and why this river received its two names, and also see if you can think of any other cases where we have two different names for the same thing, according to the place we happen to be in when we are speaking of it."

"Do *you* know of any such cases?" asked John.

"I know of one," replied Lawrence. "When we are not in the cars, we commonly call the stopping-places of the trains *dépôts*, but when we are in them we call such places *stations*. We never ask, for example, when we are traveling, 'What dépôt is this?' or say that we are going to stop at the next dépôt, but always *station*. And yet, when out of the cars, at a hotel, or in the streets of a town, people almost always say dépôt."

"That's curious," said John; "I wonder what the reason is!"

"I think there must be some reason, or at least some explanation of such a usage," replied Lawrence. "It would be a good plan for you, some time when you have nothing to do, to think of it, and see if you can study it out."

Lawrence did not think it at all necessary that he should

try to give some kind of explanation, satisfactory or otherwise, of every remarkable appearance or phenomena which
they chanced to observe, especially when the questions
which arose in connection with them related to branches
of knowledge which John, in the course of his education,
had not yet reached. He was very willing to open before
him, from time to time, glimpses of fields of investigation
to the very boundaries of which he had not yet attained.

There was a double advantage in this. In the first place,
the bringing to his view in this way curious and interesting questions connected with scenes which he had not begun to study, and of the very nature of which he had but
little idea, expanded his ideas in respect to the vast extent
of the field of knowledge which he had yet to explore, and
increased his interest in going forward. Then, in the second place, showing him the boundlessness of the field before him tended to prevent his becoming vain and conceited in thinking of the acquisitions that he had already
made.

I say only that it *tended* to produce this last good result, for it is almost impossible to accomplish it entirely.
Boys like John, who take a great interest in learning all
they can, and who, of course, make rapid progress in learning, almost always, for a time, become more or less conceited. It is not at all surprising that it should be so, since
their appreciation of what is contained within the little
field which they have already explored is necessarily so
much more vivid and distinct than any conceptions which
they can form of what is before them in the boundless regions into which they have not yet entered.

About twenty or thirty miles above New York the river
expands into a broad and spacious lake, called the Tappan
Sea.

"We are coming to the Tappan Sea," said John. "Let

us go forward, so that we can look out ahead and see the vessels on the water."

So they rose from their seats and walked through the long upper saloon to the forward part of the steam-boat. This saloon was richly decorated, carpeted, and furnished, and many groups of gentlemen and ladies were seated upon the sofas, and lounges, and comfortable chairs, and parties of children were playing together here and there upon the floor. Along the sides of the room were ranges of doors opening into the different staterooms. The room was very long, and had a very rich and elegant appearance, but the whole expression of the interior was entirely different from that of the main cabins of a sea-going steamer. There every thing is solid, massive, strong, and firmly secured; here the style was comparatively light, airy, and graceful, and to the eyes of Lawrence and John, accustomed, as they were, to the shocks, and concussions, and general rough usage which the *Scotia* or the *Cuba* had had to sustain from the billows of the Atlantic, seemed exceedingly frail.

From the forward end of this saloon Lawrence and John passed out through a door to an open part of the deck over the bows, where they had a very fine view of the grand expanse of water before them.

"What a splendid lake!" said John; "and how many steam-boats and vessels!"

"Yes," replied Lawrence; "isn't it a pity that is all going to be filled up?"

"Going to be filled up!" repeated John, much surprised; "what are they going to fill it up for?"

"*They* are not going to do it. It is the river that will do it," replied Lawrence. "The river will fill it all up, except a winding channel that it will leave through the land that it makes for its own flow. All the rest will be filled up and formed into a region of level green fields."

John was much surprised at this statement, and asked how it would be done. Lawrence explained to him that the lake was a vast hollow in the land filled with water, and that the river was all the time bringing down sand, and pebbles, and sediments of various kinds from the country above; and that, though some of these materials were carried through and borne out through the lower end of the lake, and so onward into the sea, some portion must necessarily be left behind, and in process of time the whole lake must be filled.

"Nonsense!" said John; "such a great lake as this could *never* be filled in this way. There would not be sediment enough brought down to fill it—not in a thousand years!"

"Perhaps not," said Lawrence; "but if the river could not fill it in a thousand years, it might in ten thousand."

"No," rejoined John, "I don't believe it would fill it even in ten thousand."

"Then ten million," replied Lawrence. "You can have as many years as you want. There are plenty of them coming. If there is any deposit at all left in the lake, and nothing to take it away, the lake must some time or other become filled up."

The conversation on this subject was continued between Lawrence and John for some time, and in the course of it Lawrence explained somewhat at length the manner in which natural depressions in the surface of the land which occur in the course of the current of a river, or widenings of the valley through which it flows, and which at first become, of course, so many reservoirs of water supplied by the river, thus forming lakes, are gradually filled up by deposits of sand and soil, so as to form in the end broad plains bordering the river, covered with verdure and trees, and with a tortuous channel through the centre of them kept open for the passage of the water.

The process is a very curious one, and has been observed, and the different steps of the progress of it in particular instances have been carefully noted and recorded by men of science.

The philosophy of the operation is this: All rivers in their flow bring down with them a great deal of sediment-ary matter, which results in part from the disintegration of the rocks and mountains among which their several branches take their rise, and also from dust blown into them by the wind, and from decayed animal and vegetable substances brought into them by the rains.

The heavier portions of these substances sink rapidly, and are rolled along the bottoms of the rivers in the form of pebbles and sand. Those that are not so heavy sink more slowly, and where the flow of the stream is rapid and turbulent, their complete subsidence is entirely prevented by the surging and whirl of the water; and in general, the tendency to subsidence on the part of the solid matter held in suspension is determined in a great measure by the slowness or swiftness of the current.

Now, in all those places where the river is very broad and deep, the motion of the water is very slow, on account of the space through which it moves being so vast, and the quantity moving being so great, that the whole amount that has to pass through during a given time can be trans-mitted by a very slow motion.

Of course, in all those places where the space is so wide and deep as to form a lake, the deposition takes place much more rapidly than in other places; and, unless something interferes with the process, the lake, after a certain time, becomes entirely filled up.

"Then I don't see," said John, when Lawrence had arrived at this point in his explanation, "how any channel is left for the passage of the water."

"There is something very curious and remarkable about that," replied Lawrence. "You see that the tendency to deposit is greatest where the water is most nearly in a state of repose, and least along the line of swiftest motion. Where this line of swiftest motion would be would depend much upon the conformation of the shores, but it would in general tend to pass somewhere through the middle of the lake. Of course, as the progress of the deposition goes on nearer the shores and in all the stiller portions of the water, the space which the whole volume of the water will have for its flow will be more and more contracted, and the current along it will become swifter and swifter, and thus, as the channel becomes contracted and defined, there will be an increasing force in the flow of the water to keep it from being closed entirely.

"At last," continued Lawrence, "things would come in such a case into a state of equilibrium—that is, the tendency of the sediment to subside through the water by its weight, and to be borne onward by the swiftness of the current, would balance each other, and the channel of the river would then become in some measure permanent as to its size—that is, as to what is called the area of its section, only now, instead of forming a lake, it would flow meanderingly through a level plain, over which every freshet would deposit a fresh layer of fertilizing soil, until it was raised far above the level of the ordinary flow of the river."

Lawrence went on farther to explain that this process of filling up all the natural depressions in the land through which rivers flow, and which originally formed the beds of lakes, had been going on for thousands of years, and

N

that there were now found along the courses of all rivers a great many places where, according to every appearance, there had formerly been depressions which the river originally filled with water, so as to form lakes and ponds, but which are now filled up nearly to the height of the highest freshets, and have become smooth and level plains, covered with grass and trees. Such grounds as these are called meadows and intervals, and sometimes river bottoms. The river flows through these fluviatile lands—that is, river-made lands, by a very devious and winding channel, which is continually changing.

"Why does not it flow straight, and keep always to the same channel?" asked John.

"Ah! that is a very important question," replied Lawrence, "though I have not time to explain the case to you now, for it is about time for the gong to sound for tea. We shall have an excellent opportunity to study the operation of the water in a river channel at Carlton, when we get there, for you remember the river twists and winds about there through the meadows in front of our house, and wears away the banks on one side or the other incessantly."

"Yes," replied John, "it twines about in great sweeps, and the banks in the hollow of the sweeps are caving in."

"It is almost always so," rejoined Lawrence, "with the course of a river through the lands which it has made itself. There is a splendid opportunity to see this from the top of Mount Holyoke, where we look down upon a region which seems once to have been a great lake, but which now consists of a plain formed of the most fertile and beautiful meadows in the world, the river flowing through them with the most extraordinary windings."

The engraving gives us a glimpse of these lands, and of the windings of the river through them, as seen from near

ANCIENT LAKE FILLED UP.

the summit of Mount Holyoke. It presents to our view a very perfect example of an ancient lake filled up, and the river flowing through the new ground in a tortuous channel.

"Are we going by Mount Holyoke on our way home?" asked John.

"We are going pretty near to it," said Lawrence.

"Then let us stop and go up," said John; "I like to climb mountains and see the views."

"Very well," replied Lawrence. "The view from Mount Holyoke is very beautiful, and it is very instructive, too, for one who is studying these subjects. But we can see the operation of the process to better advantage at Carlton, for there every thing is on a smaller scale, and the changes are more perceptible. The great principles are the same in all cases, from the smallest brooks to the mightiest rivers. But why does not the gong sound?"

"I wish it would sound," replied John, "for I'm hungry for supper."

"The general principle is this," resumed Lawrence, reverting to the subject of the flow of rivers: "The true and ultimate function of brooks and rivers is to *remove the mountains to the sea!* Of course they can not carry them down whole, but the frost, and the ice, and the rain disintegrate and wear away the rocks, and deliver the materials into the streams in such a form that the water can carry them on. The river first employs these materials in filling up all the hollows and depressions in the ground that it meets with on its way. But it does not leave any single portion of them long there, for, by twisting and winding in its course, it continually washes away and carries down the stream successive portions of the land it formed years before, and replaces what is thus removed from one side of the river by new formations, which it gradually builds up

on the other side from fresh materials.   We shall be able
to see all this work going on, upon a comparatively small
scale, when we get to Carlton."

Carlton was the name which I give to the town where
Lawrence and John lived.   It was situated among the
mountains in the interior of New England.

"I mean to watch the river when I get home," said John,
"and see how it works."

"You can even do more than that," rejoined Lawrence;
"you can actually experiment with a stream yourself, if
you take one small enough; for the laws which govern the
flow of water, and the transportation of solid matter sus-
pended in it, or borne along by it, are the same, and the
effects that result are analogous, whatever is the size of
the stream; only in the smaller streams the changes are
more rapid, and being, moreover, comprised within a nar-
rower area, are more easy of observation."

"Yes," said John, "there's the Beaver Brook, where I
used to have my dam.   I mean to go and see how it is on
the Beaver Brook as soon as I get home."

The conversation on this subject was here suddenly interrupted by the sound of the gong, on hearing which John
rose at once with great alacrity, and, followed by Lawrence,
went down to supper.   He, however, did not forget what
Lawrence had explained to him about the action of rivers
in filling up such natural depressions in the land as came
in their course, and forming green and fertile meadows in
the places they had occupied, nor the resolution which he
had made to investigate the subject by observations and
experiments upon the streams in the neighborhood when
he should reach home.   An account of the results of these
observations and experiments will be contained in the next
volume of this series, which is to be entitled WATER AND
LAND.

CHAPTER XXXI.

LIGHTING BY GAS.

The sun had gone down and the twilight was far advanced before the gong was sounded which summoned the passengers on board the steamer to supper, and when Lawrence and John went below they found the supper-tables lighted by a long row of candles.

"Why don't they light the cabin with gas?" asked John, as soon as they were seated at the table. "Oh! I might have known myself," he added, after a moment's reflection; "they could not bring the pipes on board."

"True," replied Lawrence, "they could not bring the gas in by pipes from the mains in the city, but there are other ways in which we can conceive of gas being brought on board a steamer besides drawing it from the great city gasometers. In the form in which it exists in these gasometers, it is altogether too much expanded and too bulky to be conveniently transported or stored, but there are two modes of bringing it in a more compact form: first, by introducing it in what may be called the *original packages*, and, secondly, by packing it anew expressly for the purpose."

John did not know at all what Lawrence meant by this language. He did not understand, he said, how such a substance as gas could be packed at all. So Lawrence explained to him what he meant. He did this in conversation which was partly held at the supper-table, and partly afterward in the saloon above, when they went up after the supper was concluded. The substance of the conversation was this:

One would not suppose that such a substance as gas could be packed very easily in any way, and yet Nature has the art of stowing it in a very compact form in all that class of substances which have already been described as *hydrocarbons*—that is to say, in almost all natural substances that are inflammable. It is packed very closely in wood, in all bituminous coal, and in all such substances as resin, pitch, wax, and tallow.

"Indeed," said Lawrence, pointing to one of the tall candles which stood upon the table before them while they were at supper, "providing these candles is only a mode of bringing gas on board in a compact and manageable form. The paraffine of which these candles are made is a hydrocarbon—that is, it is composed chiefly of hydrogen and carbon combined with each other and packed very closely together. The heat of the burning wick liberates them and restores them to their gaseous form, and they then burn, just as the gas in the cities does from a jet; only, in the case of the candle, the gas is burned directly as fast as it is set free, and in the place where it is set free, instead of being saved and stored in a great reservoir, and then conveyed in pipes to be burned in different places at a distance from where it is produced. In a philosophical point of view, and in all essential respects, the burning of a candle is the same as burning gas from a jet."

"That's curious," said John; "and is it the same with a lamp?"

"Precisely the same," replied Lawrence; "only, in the case of the lamp, the material from which the gas is distilled is a liquid, instead of being a solid, as it is in the case of the candle.

"Thus, in point of fact," continued Lawrence, "they do burn gas in this steamer. They bring it on board packed very snugly in the paraffine of the candles. They might, even, in fact, bring it packed in coal, were it not for the inconvenience they would incur in that case in the work of unpacking it."

In speaking thus of hydrogen and carbon, which are the constituents of illuminating gas, as *packed* in paraffine and in coal, Lawrence used language, it must be confessed, in a somewhat figurative sense; but these materials do certainly exist in these substances in a very highly condensed and concentrated condition. Indeed, Nature seems to have the power of carrying into effect this kind of packing in a most extraordinary degree.

Water, for example, is composed of the two substances oxygen and hydrogen, both of which in their ordinary condition, as known to us, appear in the form of a gas. Nature, in combining these substances in the form of water, brings enormous volumes of them into very small compass, and retains them in that condition without any external force of compression or any means of confinement whatever. Man can not produce this condensation by a pressure of a hundred and fifty atmospheres.

I shall presently explain what is meant by an *atmosphere* as a measure of pressure, though the explanation will not help the reader to form any distinct conception of what a pressure of a hundred and fifty atmospheres is, as no one can form any adequate idea of such enormous forces except those who have witnessed the production of them and observed practically some of their effects.

Somewhat in the same way by which the powers of nature hold the naturally gaseous substances of oxygen and hydrogen in so very compact and concentrated a condition in water, do they also hold the carbureted hydrogen in the paraffine of the candle and in coal. In the case of coal, the quantity held within a given space varies much, according to the different qualities of the coal, and to other circum-

stances; but it is not uncommon to find a quantity of illuminating gas sufficient to fill a room thirty feet square
and ten feet high so closely compressed in the coal containing it, that if, while it was in that state, it could be
separated from the other constituents of the coal, it would
form a solid block which a man could easily lift.

Thus, as Lawrence said, bringing the gas on board the
vessel packed in paraffine or in coal is altogether a more
convenient mode than to attempt to bring it in pure, in its
natural form and of its natural bulk, as gas. In the form
of paraffine it is much more expensive, in the first instance,
than as one of the constituents of coal, but then it is much
more easily extracted, or, perhaps, it would be better to
say, developed, from that substance than from coal; for,
in the case of paraffine, or wax, or tallow, or any other such
substance, all that is necessary is to have a wick passing
up through it and set on fire, and the process of melting
successive portions of the substance, and converting them
into an illuminating gas, goes on of itself, without any apparatus or machinery whatever.

Whereas, on the other hand, although people might obtain the necessary supply of gas in *coal* cheaper than in
any of those other forms, there would be required a complicated, and expensive, and bulky, and even somewhat
dangerous apparatus to distill it. There would have to be
a furnace to heat the coal, and tight iron retorts to contain
it so as to prevent the gas from being burned in the furnace as fast as it was produced, and a reservoir to store it,
and pipes to convey it to the different parts of the vessel
where it might be required, all of which would involve
much trouble and expense.

"That would not do at all," said John, when Lawrence
explained these things to him.

"Especially," he added, after thinking a moment, "in

the case of a steamer at sea, tossing and pitching about in a storm."

Besides these objections which Lawrence pointed out, we may add that the process of preparing gas from coal, or, as Lawrence called it, the work of "unpacking it," not only involves the use of complicated machinery, but requires skilled workmen to manage the machinery and to conduct the process. And these men must devote, too, all their time to the work, and must be well paid, so that it is, on every account, much better to produce the gas for illumination from some of the substances that can be used in the form of candles or in lamps, though they cost more at the outset. It is only when very large quantities of gas are required, and in places, too, where there is ample room for all the machinery and appointments, that it can be profitably obtained from coal.

Thus it can be manufactured advantageously on a great scale for lighting cities and towns, and even for extensive private establishments where there is plenty of space at command for the necessary works; but for single dwellings, or small establishments of every kind, if they are to be lighted artificially at all, the gas must be brought in packed, as Lawrence called it, in paraffine, or wax, or spermaceti, or tallow, or oil, or kerosene, or some other similar hydrocarbon.

"I never thought before," remarked John, when Lawrence had made these explanations to him, "that, when we were burning lamps or candles, we were really burning gas."

"Yes," replied Lawrence; "what is actually burnt in both cases is essentially the same, only, in the case of a candle or lamp, the gas is burned as fast as it is set free, while in the case of regular gas-works it is kept from being burned for a time after it is set free, and is conveyed

in pipes wherever the light from it is wanted. Even the
flame of burning wood from a fire is the flame of gas, you
recollect."

"I remember you told me once," replied John, "how I
might draw it off from the fire through a pipe-stem, and
burn it at the end of the stem."

"Yes," rejoined Lawrence; "and we might easily draw
it off farther than that, if we chose, by means of an India-
rubber tube.

"Only, in that case," added Lawrence, "it would be better to take some other larger and stronger receptacle than
the bowl of a pipe for a retort—a gun-barrel, for instance.
Chemists employ gun-barrels very often for such experiments. An old gun-barrel which is past service for shoot-
ing, such as can generally be obtained at a gunsmith's, will
make a very good retort for such purposes."

Lawrence went on to explain that, by taking such a gun-
barrel, and, after plugging up the touch-hole, filling it half
full of some hydrocarbon and connecting a long India-rubber tube with the outer end of it, the gas could be conveyed away to any distance—to a stand of some kind, for
example, upon a table in the middle of a room—and there
burned just like gas from a pipe laid in the street.

John said that he should like very much to see that
done.

"Very well," replied Lawrence; "we can do it, or, rather, you can do it yourself under my direction, when we get
home. I mean to fit up a little laboratory and workshop
in Carlton, and you can then perform as many such experiments as you like."

"I mean to make some gas, at any rate, for one thing,"
replied John. "Only," he added, after reflecting a moment, "I should think that the end of the India-rubber
tube, where it is slipped over the end of the gun-barrel,

would begin to melt or burn pretty soon. You see, if the butt end of the barrel was in the burning coals, the muzzle end would get quite hot in a very short time."

"Certainly," replied Lawrence, "unless we devised some way to keep it cool. There are a great many practical difficulties of this kind to be encountered in making chemical experiments, and it requires sometimes a good deal of ingenuity to contrive means to surmount them. That is one reason why making chemical experiments is so useful to a boy so soon as he is old enough for such work. It sharpens his wits.

"As to keeping the end of the gun-barrel cool," continued Lawrence, "there is a simple mode of doing that. We have only to wrap the outer end of the barrel, where the India-rubber tube joins it, with a strip of cotton cloth, winding it round and round in the form of a bandage, and then keeping the cloth wet by pouring on a little water from time to time out of a pitcher."

"Yes," replied John, "that would keep it cool."

"Water has a wonderful power to keep any thing cool," said Lawrence, "even though it is hot water."

"That is very strange," said John.

"I mean," said Lawrence, "to keep any thing from getting *very* hot—red hot, or hot enough to melt or burn India-rubber, for example; for, before the iron around which the wet cloth is bound becomes hot enough for that, it will be hot enough to boil the water, and water absorbs such an enormous quantity of heat in boiling as to keep the temperature of the iron down to a comparative low point. Of course, as fast as the water in the cloth is boiled and converted into steam, you must pour on more, so as to keep the cloth all the time wet."

"That would be a great deal of trouble," said John.

"Yes," replied Lawrence, "and there would be a great

many other troubles and inconveniences in the attempt to produce gas on a small scale for any practical purposes, but we might be willing to take the trouble once for the sake of performing the experiment."

" Oh yes," replied John; " and I mean to try it if you will help me. I mean to have a small pitcher and pour a little water on every few minutes."

Before leaving this subject of the management of gas, I will add that there is an artificial mode of packing this bulky commodity after it is evolved, by *compressing* it, with great force, in metallic reservoirs made prodigiously strong to resist the pressure. The gas is driven into these reservoirs by means of forcing-pumps working with great power. The French have adopted this system in Paris to a considerable extent. The engraving represents a wagon loaded with gas thus compressed.

The interior of the wagon is occupied by nine cylinders, which are made of copper, and are of enormous strength. There is forced into each cylinder ten or twelve times as much gas as it would naturally contain if the gas were of its ordinary density; and as the expansive pressure of the gas is in proportion to the quantity of it that is forced into a given space, the whole interior surface of each cylinder has a force pressing upon it from within outward, and so tending to burst it, of *ten or twelve atmospheres!*

For you must understand that pressure in mechanics is measured by *atmospheres.* The pressure of the atmosphere is reckoned at fifteen pounds to the square inch. The actual pressure of the atmosphere varies from day to day in the same place according to the quantity of air that there may happen to be for the time being over the place, and in different places according to their elevation above the level of the sea; but fifteen pounds to the square inch is taken as the standard of measurement, or, in other words,

A WAGON-LOAD OF GAS

fifteen pounds to the square inch is an *atmosphere of press-ure.* This is a fundamental principle or fact which it is very important to remember. It comes continually into philosophical and mechanical calculations.

The meaning of the principle thus stated is, that, light and rare as the atmosphere seems to us, in moving through it, it extends to so great a height above the surface of the earth, and the quantity is in the whole so great, that the weight of it is equal to fifteen pounds upon every square inch that it presses upon. That is to say, if you place a small block of wood an inch square upon a table, and a fif-teen pound weight upon the block, the additional pressure would be that of *one atmosphere;* and this additional press-ure would be just equal to the original pressure of the at-mosphere itself, so that, with the pressure of the weight, the whole pressure would be exactly doubled.

Now this original pressure, great as it is, is not felt by us, because it acts in every direction; just as a fish swim-ming in the water does not feel the weight of the water over him, because, the water being so perfect a fluid, the pressure resulting from the weight diffuses itself and bal-ances itself in every direction, so that the fish floats in it, as it were—in the pressure, I mean, not the water—and is not sensible of it at all; so we ourselves float, as it were, in the pressure of the air, which acts from above and be-low, upon every substance and upon every side of it, equal-ly, and even from the pores and interstices within it out-wardly, so that it produces, in ordinary cases, no percepti-ble effect. The amount of it, however, in every direction and from every side, is fifteen pounds to the square inch.

Now this pressure is really much greater than one would at first imagine. The surface of one side of a man's hand, for example, contains not less, including the fingers, than twenty square inches; consequently, the weight of the air pressing upon the hand when the man holds it out horizontally before him is not less than twenty times fifteen pounds—that is, three hundred pounds! Now, if this downward pressure upon the upper surface were not balanced and counteracted by an equal upward pressure upon the under surface, and also from certain resisting pressures exerted by the fluids within the hand, no man could hold his hand out horizontally in that manner for a moment.

We see what the prodigious force of this pressure is, when not counterbalanced, by the action of certain steam-engines which are worked on the principle of producing a vacuum upon each side of the piston in the cylinder alternately, by which means the counterbalancing pressure is taken off, and the pressure of the air on the other side is allowed to act without any thing to oppose it. By this means the piston is driven to and fro with prodigious force, developing a power that is sufficient to work the heaviest machinery, and all by the simple pressure of the atmosphere upon one side of the piston when the balancing resistance on the other side is taken away.

And yet this is only the pressure of *one* atmosphere. It is precisely this amount of pressure which is exerted both on the inside and on the outside of a glass bottle, or any other receptacle the interior of which has an open and free communication with the outside air.

If, however, this free communication is closed, and a double quantity of air is forced into the receptacle through a pipe fitted to it for the purpose, then we should have the pressure of two atmospheres on the inside and only one on the outside, and there would be a surplus force of fifteen pounds upon every square inch of the internal surface, tending to burst the vessel. If treble the quantity were introduced, then there would be a preponderance of two atmospheres—that is, of *thirty* pounds to the square inch. This amount of pressure on every square inch of a vessel of the size of a barrel, for example, would constitute an enormous bursting force—a force of forty or fifty thousand pounds!

It is on this principle, however, that the copper cylinders in the gas wagon shown in the engraving were filled, and yet so prodigiously heavy and strong were they made, that sometimes, as has already been said, *ten* or *twelve* volumes of gas were forced into them. If the number is taken as eleven, then, allowing one to balance the ordinary atmospheric pressure on the outside, we should have an expansive force of *a hundred and fifty pounds* to the square inch acting all the time upon the interior surfaces of all the cylinders.

The gas, in this compact form, was conveyed about the city and delivered to the consumers. Those who chose to take their gas of this company, of course, were obliged to provide the means of receiving it in the form of a gasometer, or of some very strong and well-secured receptacle, for the cylinders in the wagon were altogether too massive, solid, and heavy to be removed. When the wagon arrived at the door of one of the customers, a pipe from one of the cylinders in the wagon was connected with one communicating with the reservoir within, and then, when the stopcock was open, the gas from the cylinder would rush in by its own expansive force until the quantity in the two receptacles was equal—that is, in case the receptacles themselves were equal—and the pressure would be that of five atmospheres in each.

Then, of course, no more would flow from that cylinder, but an additional quantity could be thrown in from a fresh cylinder where the pressure of the whole ten atmospheres was still entire. The first cylinder, moreover, which had delivered half its gas, could be made to deliver more at the establishment of the next customer, whose receptacle, being empty, would be ready to take half of that which still remained. Thus, while the cylinder in the wagon would deliver five atmospheres at the first customer's, it would deliver two and a half, which would be half of the remainder, at the second, and so on. In this way, with proper management, a large portion of the load could be delivered, and the residue, which was not delivered, would not be lost, but would remain in the cylinders as so much toward the next filling.

The plan, however, after all, was not found to be practically successful. There were so many difficulties and incumbrances to interfere with the easy and convenient management of it that it never was carried into extensive operation. One good, however, results from the experiment: it affords an excellent illustration to aid the young student to understand the nature and the operation of *pressures*, and the modes of measuring them, and Lawrence made very good use of it for this purpose in his conversation with John.

CHAPTER XXXII.

CONCLUSION.

THE steamer by which Lawrence and John made their passage up the North River arrived at Albany early in the morning. From Albany they were to continue their journey by land. Their route lay to the eastward, toward New England. The scenery along the road was very picturesque and beautiful, and the locomotive, as if equally proud of the large company of neatly-dressed passengers under his charge, filling the long train of cars which he

THE LOCOMOTIVE.

had to draw, and of the beauty of the country through
which he had to take them, ran whistling along his way
as if his heart was filled with gladness and joy, now
winding around the point of a rocky hill, now running
with redoubled speed down a long incline, but always
bringing, at every moment, new scenes of fertility and
beauty into view—smiling valleys, pretty towns, and for-
est-covered hills.

John was much interested, as they went on, in observing
all the streams flowing through the valleys which they
could overlook from the windows of the car, and he saw
many examples of such streams pursuing a very meander-
ing course through level meadow-lands, which had every
appearance of having been formed by the filling up of ancient lakes or ponds. The case in which this effect was
manifested on the grandest scale was that of the windings
of the Connecticut River at the foot of Mount Holyoke.
The travelers stopped over one train expressly to obtain
a good view of this valley, which object they attained by
going partly up Mount Holyoke. They did not have time
to go to the top.

When at length they took their places in the train again
to resume their journey, John amused himself with reading
for a time, and then finally shut his book and said he was
very tired.

"I suppose you did not sleep very well last night on
board the steam-boat," said Lawrence; "and, besides, we
have had a somewhat fatiguing time of it to-day."

So Lawrence proposed that John should place himself in
a comfortable position and see if he could not go to sleep.
John said he was sure he could not go to sleep, for he was
not sleepy.

"You can put yourself in a comfortable position, at any
rate," said Lawrence, "and then I will tell you a story."

John said that that was exactly what he should like. So he placed his feet upon the valise, and leaned his head upon Lawrence's shoulder, and Lawrence began :

"I'll tell you the story," said he, "of the man who first discovered the mode of lighting by gas. His name was Lebon. He was a Frenchman, and an engineer by profession. He was in the government employ, being engaged in superintending certain public works and manufactures. But, besides his regular business, he was greatly interested in making investigations and experiments."

"That was a good thing," said John.

"Yes," replied Lawrence, "if it was not carried too far. He was charged with neglecting his regular duties in order to gain time to make his experiments. I do not know whether the charge was just or not, but I advise you, if you make any experiments this winter, not to let them interfere with your regular studies."

John did not answer. The truth was, he was beginning to feel a little sleepy.

"The first experiment that he made in relation to gas," continued Lawrence, "was something like our plan of distilling gas in a pipe, only he used a glass bottle instead of a pipe. He observed, in watching the fire, that the flame sometimes seemed to flicker in the air at a little distance from the wood, and he conceived the idea of separating it entirely. So he filled a glass bottle with sawdust, and fitted some kind of a tube into the mouth of it, and then put the bottle into the fire among the burning coals."

"But, Lawrence," said John, partially arousing himself, "the bottle would break."

"Yes," said Lawrence, "if he put it in suddenly it would break, but you can heat glass very hot if you heat it very gradually, and Lebon, no doubt, took all necessary precautions. His experiment succeeded very well. Then he tried

it on a larger scale; but the gas, as he first formed it, had
many impurities combined with it which gave it a bad
smell. He had a great deal of trouble in contriving modes
of freeing it from these impurities, but he succeeded tolerably well at last.

"He had, however, a great many difficulties to contend
with. His salary was very small, and the condition of the
government at that time in France was so unsettled, that
what was due him was very slowly and irregularly paid.
All his friends and acquaintances laughed at him, too, as a
visionary schemer.

"He, however, persevered, and at length succeeded in
getting his invention so far perfected that he constructed
an apparatus sufficient for lighting a house which he hired
for the purpose, and then he advertised his plan and opened
his house once a week or so to the public, on the payment
of three francs admission. Do you remember how much
three francs is, of our money?"

John did not answer.

"I verily believe the boy is asleep," said Lawrence, speaking to himself; "so much the better. Sleep will do him
more good than any story."

So Lawrence did not disturb him, but let him sleep on,
and John did not wake until he so nearly reached home
that he did not ask for the rest of the story. I will, however, add that poor Lebon did not live to see the final success of his invention. In the midst of his active efforts to
induce the government to make arrangements for giving
his new mode of illumination a fair trial on a proper scale,
he was found one morning murdered in a public park in
Paris, or, rather, in a wood which has since become a public park of great celebrity, but which was in those days des-
olate and lonely, and the resort of thieves and robbers. It
was supposed that, in crossing this ground on his way to

his home, he was waylaid and killed by the highwaymen that infested the place at night, on account of its very darkness and obscurity.

He lost his life thus for want of the safeguard in lonesome places which simple illumination affords—a safeguard which in those days could not be provided, but which, through his discoveries, was soon to be introduced into all the principal cities of the world.

Indeed, in every sense of the word, one of the greatest means of protection for the community against the prevalence and the consequences of vice and crime is Light.

Early in the evening Lawrence and John arrived safely at their respective homes.

O

THE END.

www.ingramcontent.com/pod-product-compliance
Lightning Source LLC
Chambersburg PA
CBHW031400270326
41929CB00010BA/1266